Belinda Mackie works as a psychoanalyst in private practice in Melbourne, Australia and consults in the area of addictions at Arrow Health. She completed her PhD at Monash University in 2012 and her first book, *Treating people with psychosis in institutions*, was published by Karnac (now Taylor & Francis) London in 2016.

The two most important days in your life are the day you were born, and the day you find out why.

— Marc Twain

THE GOOD NO

Belinda Mackie

Copyright © 2022 Belinda Mackie

All rights reserved.

No part of this book may be reproduced in any form or by any electronic or mechanical means including information storage and retrieval systems, without permission in writing from the Publisher.

Publishers:
Inspiring Publishers
P.O. Box 159
Calwell ACT 2905, Australia.
Email: inspiringpublishers@gmail.com

National Library of Australia Cataloguing-in-Publication entry

Author: Belinda Mackie

Title: **THE GOOD NO**

ISBN: 978-1-922792-48-8 (Print)

ISBN: 978-1-922792-49-5 (eBook)

Dedication

This book is dedicated to my brother Cameron
who could never say NO.
He died prematurely because of it on 6th June 2021.

Table of Contents

Preface xi
Introduction xiii
Chapter outline xvii
Chapter 1: The power of the good no 1
  What does NO mean? 3
  What is The Good No? 5
    Courage 7
    The Good No Formula 9
    The Good No in practice 12
Chapter 2: What interferes with The Good No? 15
  Fear 17
    FOMO 20
  The Tyranny of Niceness 20
    Toxic positivity 21
    Nice girl syndrome 25
    The soft touch 27
  People Pleasers 32
    Don't rock the boat 34
    Too good to be true 36
    Altruism and Self-sacrifice 37

Chapter 3: Why do I say Yes when I know I should say No?... 44
- Addiction ... 48
  - The Internet and Social media ... 50
- Intimacy ... 52
  - Sex, Romance and Co-dependency ... 54
  - Consent and the meaning of NO ... 59
- The Beauty Industry ... 63

Chapter 4: Healthy Mind and The Good No ... 71
- Personal ethics and values ... 73
- The Superego ... 75
  - Self-criticism ... 77
  - Self-pity ... 81
  - Overachievers ... 82
  - Faking it ... 84
- Stereotypes ... 86
  - Toxic masculinity ... 89

Chapter 5: The people you can't say NO to ... 93
- Relationships ... 94
  - Bad friends ... 97
- The Family Drama ... 100
  - Saying NO to your child ... 104

Chapter 6: Those who won't take No for an answer ... 108
- One-upmanship ... 109
- Narcissists and Control Freaks ... 111
- Emotional vampires ... 112
- People who go too far ... 114

Table of Contents

Passive-Aggression 118

Aggression and Verbal Abuse 121

CHAPTER 7: HOW DO YOU KNOW WHAT YOU ARE IN CONTROL OF? 126

Develop some skills 128

Be assertive 130

Set boundaries 131

Upholding Your rights 134

Deal with your emotions 136

Grow your Self-discipline 139

CHAPTER 8: SELF-KNOWLEDGE IS THE ONLY ANSWER 145

Discernment 147

Authenticity 149

Philosophy of life 153

Human suffering 155

Acceptance 157

Finale 160

REFERENCES 162

Preface

The background to this book is located in the many years I have come across people in my private practice, as a psychoanalyst and elsewhere, who could not say NO to the unfair or inappropriate requests and expectations of others. This means being able to say NO to yourself when you are out of line as well. In giving way to others all the time or not representing yourself authentically you let yourself down. In other words, you may be easily led, don't want to make a fuss, think saying NO is rude, are weak and avoidant, are afraid and disempowered, don't feel you are worth it, or just plain have no gumption. You could also be an addict who can't say NO to save yourself. We all suffer from human frailty, so we all make mistakes frequently, but it's challenging to watch someone who repeatedly acts in ways that are opposite to their stated desire.

To all of you who find it hard, or nearly impossible, to say NO to others I am offering a different way of understanding why you might do this, and I am proposing a few alternate ideas around how to deal with it. I have pulled thoughts and experiences from a range of sources and brought them together in a straightforward way to make some sense of this phenomenon. This book does not offer a quick fix because that would be deceptive. There is no quick fix for ingrained behaviour and beliefs that become entrenched over time and interfere with the way you live. What is expected is that you might put some effort into thinking about these issues and ponder their impact on your life. If you decide to experiment with doing some things differently, that's great. Ultimately change is your choice; it's in your hands.

I have been careful to create fictitious vignettes although certain aspects are based on real people and their common human experiences and struggles. These examples are about no one - and they are about everyone. The chapters of this book cover the nature of The Good NO, the people who need to say the good NO, the people who need to hear the good NO, the consequences of not saying the good NO, and what all of that might mean.

▶▶▶
Introduction

Being able to say NO with tact and diplomacy is the essence of *The Good NO*. However, it's not as simple as that because we have to consider the multiple reasons why saying NO and behaving in a way that's consistent with that NO is quite difficult for most people. To really know what you want requires self-knowledge, and the degree of self-knowledge you have influences who you are in the world and how you experience yourself in relation to others. It was Socrates who said *To know thyself is the beginning of wisdom*. But the road to self-knowledge is a long and rocky one. For most of us we learn that quick fixes do not shift deep-seated psychological issues and that suffering is a universal experience. It follows that as you come to know and understand yourself better you come to know and understand others as well. It is from this position of self-awareness that you might be able to discern something about what you want.

People pleasers, yes sayers and avoiders have great difficulty saying NO to the people they desire to please. The ability to say NO not only helps you to not do things that you don't want to do, it's also a deciding factor as to whether or not you want to commit to a task or to achieve certain goals. Moreover, the word NO helps you to stick with your values and principles. In the word NO lies great power, but in order to exercise this power it is essential to see the workings of the good NO and to understand how applying NO more frequently and in the right ways can enhance your life. So to know how to say NO you need to kNOw how.

Hopefully as you age you become more mature and aware that you have choices and are capable of making your own decisions, which include knowing the difference between wrong and right. Even though it takes some effort to rehabilitate the concept of NO we need to convert it into a self-respecting, honourable word ready for everyday use. Therefore, NO should not be a word that's off limits. It ought to be something that you elect to say based on your own discretion that's part of your day-to-day lexicon.

Human Rights Commission Report

On 5th March 2021 the Australian Government established an Independent Review into Commonwealth Parliamentary Workplaces. The Australian Human Rights Commission, led by the Sex Discrimination Commissioner conducted the review where contributions were received from 1723 individuals and 33 organisations. The review examined the culture of Commonwealth Parliamentary Workplaces in response to reports of bullying, sexual harassment and sexual assault. These behaviours in Australia's parliamentary workplaces have negative effects and cause significant harm to an individual's physical and mental health. Substantial and very real costs of this kind of misconduct are also borne by the workplace and community as a whole.

The report (Australian Human Rights Commission, 2021) is the first step in working out how to say NO to endemic systems of abuse that are embedded in the heart of organisations that govern this country. These are ways of operating that have been tolerated as acceptable forms of behaviour and so sanctioned at the highest levels. The Commission's report identified the drivers and risk factors associated with these unacceptable behaviours as follows:

- **The role of power**
  Participants observed that it is the misuse of power, fear of those who hold power, and a sense of entitlement that is particularly problematic.

Introduction

The Commission heard that power, including power imbalances and the misuse of power, is one of the primary drivers of misconduct in Commonwealth parliamentary workplaces.

- **Gender inequality**
  Gender inequality is also a key driver of bullying, sexual harassment and sexual assault within Commonwealth parliamentary workplaces. The Commission heard that institutional structures, processes and practices across Commonwealth parliamentary workplaces devalue women and consequently foster gendered misconduct.

- **Lack of accountability**
  Rather than being held accountable, participants told the Commission that people who engaged in misconduct were often rewarded in spite of their behaviour.

- **Entitlement and exclusion**
  A lack of diversity, the privilege of some groups of people, and the marginalisation and exclusion of others meant that certain groups were more vulnerable to misconduct, as well as, specific and unique experiences of discrimination, bullying, sexual harassment and sexual assault. Participants shared that identifying as different from the norm in these workplaces was inherently unsafe and identified a need to increase diversity to reduce the potential for people to be targeted.

Men more frequently perpetrated sexual harassment while women were more likely to bully. Those who bully or sexually harass people were likely to perpetrate these behaviours with multiple victims. The Commission consistently heard from participants throughout the review that there was considerable hesitancy and fear about making a complaint or report. Some people described feeling that the only options were to tolerate the misconduct or leave their job, rather than expecting that the misconduct could be addressed. Many also described the negative personal and career consequences that they experienced as a result of making a complaint.

The challenge of effectively preventing and responding to bullying, sexual harassment and sexual assault in these workplaces is significant. The proposed Framework for Action in the Report provides a substantial program of reform, which requires a sustained focus to achieve full implementation and strong leadership is critical to its success. In fact, what it needs is a strong and sustained good NO, which translates as zero tolerance of bullying, sexual harassment and sexual assault. The question is how prepared are we to stand up and say NO when we are confronted by these behaviours, especially when they are condoned by the Government of the day. This report calls out the kind of behaviour that is unacceptable in any civilised country. At the very least naming the issue and attempting to understand it is the first step to changing it. The next step is having the courage to act on what you know.

▶▶▶
Chapter outline

The first chapter explains the power of *The Good NO* and what is required to practise it. This chapter defines the nature of what it is and elaborates its meaning and application. In order to understand how applying NO more frequently in the right ways can enhance your life you need to kNOw how to say NO and that taking a stand requires courage`.

The second chapter looks at what interferes with you saying NO when you ought to. One of the chief hindrances to representing a good NO is the tyranny of niceness and positivity that pervades our culture with its dictates of people pleasing and do-gooding. The most important thing that interferes with saying NO is fear. The chapter investigates thinking around fear and what it takes to be brave enough to consciously put yourself in the position to face your fears. The tyranny of niceness includes toxic positivity where a positive mindset should be maintained at all costs and the nice girl syndrome that's based on not being good enough or having self-respect. Being passive means being vulnerable and sooner or later being taken advantage of. Yes sayers, fence sitters, and people pleasers all say Yes to unacceptable requests based on their desire to please others. They do not want to rock the boat because they are scared. They are unable to say NO without inflicting literal or metaphorical pain upon themselves.

Next, in chapter three, we explore together the nature of addiction and why we say yes when we should be saying NO. Addiction takes the form of substance abuse, but this chapter also looks at internet and social media addiction, the beauty industry, sex addiction and co-dependency, as well as, exploring issues of what constitutes consent in the era of the *#metoo* movement. What if you always say Yes to avoid saying NO. What if saying Yes comes from a habit that you can't change. Constantly saying Yes when you want to say NO can leave you vulnerable, stressed and exhausted. The inability to say NO is often linked to addictive behaviours and this chapter is all about addiction and its consequences.

Chapter four investigates how the good NO can affect your mental health. To be able to take care of or defend ourselves against an external threat, you have to be on your own side, because if your entire personality is geared towards interpreting yourself as bad, wrong, a mistake, shameful or a piece of shit you have no stable ground to fight back from. Mental health is a key component of overall health and wellbeing. The ordinary everyday madness, to which we human beings are all subject in varying degrees, is usually formed in our earliest relationship experiences. Some of life's decisions are really about determining what you value most. When many options seem reasonable, it's helpful and comforting to rely on your values and use them as a strong guiding force to point you in the right direction. This chapter explores the nature of your conscience or superego in the form of self-criticism, and self-pity, and overachieving. It also explores why you might 'fake it' by pretending to be someone you are not and the influence of stereotypes on your outlook such as toxic masculinity.

Chapter five has a focus on the people you cannot say NO to. The kind of family you are born into has a major impact on your ability to have connected and satisfying relationships. You need to be open to your emotions and your vulnerability and be willing to tangle with unpleasant and painful truths about yourself. But what about problematic relationships you've been putting up with or side stepping. If you want anything to ever change with your family or friend drama, you will need to draw a line in the sand and stick to it with a good NO.

Chapter outline

Chapter six identifies those in your life who will not take NO for an answer. These more challenging circumstances include those people who ignore what you have said, they talk over you, they pretend they have not heard you, their talk gets louder and louder till they block you out, and in fact they will not allow your NO at all. Anyone who disregards your right to reasonably refuse is someone who does not have your best interests at heart. These are people like narcissists, emotional vampires, dictators and those who practice aggression and passive aggression. How do you leave this lot behind?

Chapter seven looks as what you are in control of rather than other people that you have no control over. You are responsible for yourself and the consequences of your actions or lack thereof. You need to develop skills in the area of setting boundaries, being assertive, protecting your rights, and dealing with your emotions. Developing self-discipline around saying NO in a good way is important.

Finally, the emphasis in chapter eight is on self-knowledge that's based on *The Good kNOw*. This requires you to see yourself from a new perspective and to cultivate an understanding of how your mind and body react to the varied and complex experiences that go on in the world around you. It's about developing your own philosophy of life based on discernment, self-discipline, authenticity and acceptance. And it's important to know that, one way or another, we all suffer. Other forms of spirituality and philosophy are introduced that offer a path to fulfilment. Understanding something about your suffering gives you the chance to make choices that are well defined and worthwhile. Your job is to find your own path.

▶▶▶

Chapter 1:
THE POWER OF THE GOOD NO

Don't you know that 'No' is the wildest word we consign to Language?
　　　　　　　　　　　　The Lord Letters (1878) by Emily Dickinson

The Good NO is a refusal or rejection that's done naturally and with subtlety. It's about acknowledging to yourself that you can't do everything and at some point you need to make choices about what you want and what you don't want. Saying NO to people is an essential part of relationships and of life. The Good NO is a refusal that's delivered to the other person with respect and diplomacy. If you demonstrate integrity in the way you relate to others it can also be said that you are representing yourself as a decent civilised human being. That means communicating with language that is clear and uncompromising in the way your messages are delivered. Learning to say NO in the right way at the right time to the right person more often than not improves that relationship. It's all about how to say what you really mean, without being mean, whenever possible in your communication with others. The spirit of The Good NO encourages you to support and sustain relationships, if you can, by being honest and considerate of others.

The bedrock of who you are is formed in your earliest relationships within your family and what you inherit from previous generations. We tend to experience interpersonal conflict because we believe that we will lose the love or goodwill of others if we do not behave in certain ways.

However, overcoming the fear of rejection by saying NO is essentially you taking control of your life. Rather than feeling trapped, resentful or guilty, making your intentions clear helps you grow a sense of freedom and empowerment instead. It's not about turning down all requests that come your way, but you do need to be discerning around what you want to say Yes to and why. This is because your Yes is valuable. So how do you do that? You say NO effectively so that you can really mean it when you say Yes.

Respectful thoughtful necessary NO's will help you live a more satisfying life that's also a lot less stressful. You experience stress when you are driven to defend an idea or to stand up for something. For some this may be quite disabling, causing them to agree to things they feel unhappy about. This leads to feelings of betrayal and resentment about the situation. This resentment can become habit forming and is reinforced when it is repeated over and over in response to the triggering situation. At some point down the track, fear will have become deeply ingrained and attached to certain situations and certain people. What is produced are varying levels of distress, and degrees of dysfunction that are kept deep inside and revealed to the outside world in the form of symptoms. The subsequent internal conflict can have catastrophic consequences in relationships and lead to symptoms of, for example, anxiety, depression or substance abuse.

You have the right to say NO. NO is a tool for honesty and change. The joy of saying NO is not about apologising for saying NO it's about deciding what your priorities are. There's no magic formula or rule to follow in saying NO. It's a personal choice. YES and NO are essential to the cycle of life. By saying NO to some things and to some people, you can say Yes to your top priorities in life, and one of them is your health and wellbeing. The good 'kNOw' is located in self-knowledge. It's about knowing what you want and what you don't want.

Chapter 1: The power of the good no

What does **NO** *mean?*

NO often has a negative connotation that's situated opposite the word Yes, which is considered a positive term. NO is used when someone is denying or rejecting something. It is used in English to express dissent or refusal, as in a response to a question or request. NO can be a determiner, an adverb, an interjection or a noun. There are numerous ways to communicate NO. Casually we might say: nope, na, nah, nup, nu-uh, negative, naw, not, no go, nix, never, zilch, zero, null, nothing, naught or nil. Other colloquialisms might be: ain't, bah, forget it, for shizzle, GTFO, hell no, NAK, negatory, not on your life, no way, shintock, yeah no, yeah right (sarcasm) and you're dreaming.

There's a definite NO in the form of: not at all, not likely, not ever, not a hope in hell, not going to happen, certainly not and never in a million years. Then there is the reasonable: I disagree, I beg to differ, I veto that and the oppositional form of NO as in: deny, reject, refuse, anti, against, forbid, prohibit, bar or ban. There are also words for NO that defend a boundary, like: stop, halt, don't go there, it's enough, do not enter, I can't, leave me alone, get out and go away.

Finally, NO can be communicated non-verbally with a distinct shake of the head from left to right, by putting your hand up in the stop gesture or by crossing both arms in front. A NO equivalent in some other languages are: in French *Non,* in German *Nein,* the Greek *Ochi,* in Arabic its *La,* the Italian and Spanish both say *No,* Icelanders say *Nei,* in Indonesian its *Tidak,* in Hindi *Nahin,* and the Chinese don't have a word for NO, but the closest word to it translates as 'wrong.'

Is saying NO really hard for you to do? If your reply to this question is a Yes, then you should read on and find out if you're one of those people who truly cannot say NO:

- You constantly say Yes to things you do not want to do.
- You always end up accepting invitations to events that you had no intention of going to.
- You are handed the bill at restaurants because everybody knows you will pay.
- You are always the designated driver.
- You clear up and wash the dishes even if you did the cooking.
- Your bargaining skills are worse than a toddler's.
- Your siblings always got what they wanted from you.
- You end up drinking more than you intended.
- You do everybody's work while they take time off.
- You lend things to people who you know will never return them.
- You have a friend who is your reminder to 'say-NO'.
- You make false promises to yourself that next time you will definitely say NO.
- You lend money to whoever asks.
- You never complain.
- Your conscience bites back at you terribly when you actually, finally manage to say NO just the one time.

Chapter 1: The power of the good no

What is The Good No?

Saying a point blank blunt NO to someone can be experienced as rude and some people may be puzzled or even offended, especially if they are used to you saying Yes all the time. However, a good NO is a refusal or rejection that's done naturally and with subtlety. Communicating with diplomacy and tact is usually the best way to proceed where your approach is polite and where honesty is recommended. Saying NO to people is an essential part of life. It's about acknowledging to yourself that you can't do everything, and if you always say Yes, you are not going to have enough time or energy to do anything else, let alone for yourself. While you don't always have to offer the other person a reason or an explanation for saying NO, it's often worth taking the time to express yourself in a friendly manner. Say what you mean, mean what you say and make your intentions clear. Leave the door open for them by offering an alternative. Overcoming your fear of rejection by saying NO is really you taking control of your life. Rather than feeling trapped, resentful, or guilty you can grow a sense of freedom and empowerment instead. NO is a little word that packs the punch of a sentence.

To start with there are a few basic things to think about. Ask yourself:

- Do I want to say Yes or No? Or can I sit this one out?
- Why do I always say Yes? Am I just saying Yes out of habit?
- Why can't I say NO? What am I afraid of? When is it okay to say NO?
- Am I being realistic or am I being neurotic?
- Will they be irreparably damaged if I say NO? Probably not!
- Do I regret saying Yes or not?

Remember the following:

- Think for yourself and make independent decisions rather than following the crowd.

- Make a decision and follow through. Resist over-thinking or procrastinating about it. Just do it!
- Learn from hindsight by weighing up the benefits and the negatives.
- Get rid of people who you are sure are wrong for you.
- Think about your resources and the waste of time, energy, love and money.
- Identify what your outer perimeter is and protect yourself with a Good NO. Set your boundaries and continually enforce those limits.
- Adding humour always helps because it relaxes you and the other person.

Saying the good NO isn't necessarily easy but it's often necessary, particularly at work and even more so in personal relationships. For example, it will always be hard to tell someone the relationship is over, but taking the coward's way out by dumping your partner via text message is unacceptable even though it's quite common these days. This approach lacks integrity. By facing the music and making a decision you take responsibility for what you have done, including the impact on the other person. This is not about judging your decision to end the relationship as wrong, but the way you conduct yourself in conveying the message. This is saying NO from a place of kNOwledge and integrity. When you are asked to take on a work project and you are already over-stretched, being able to push back without leaving the other person feeling slighted is a valuable skill. Similarly, when a friend invites you to something you're not up for, knowing how to say NO considerately preserves the connection. Taking this a step further, developing discretion and subtlety in the tone you use, especially in emails and texts, is important so the person you're saying NO to can understand that you are holding them in mind. This kind of diplomacy is central to the art of The Good NO.

Chapter 1: The power of the good no

Tact and diplomacy are skills that are communicated through the respect and thoughtfulness you show to other people. This is demonstrated in your sensitivity to the opinions, beliefs, ideas and feelings of others. Diplomacy refers to interactions with others that foster good relationships. Being diplomatic enables you to make a point fluently and succinctly without making an enemy. This involves using phrases to soften your speech when you deliver a negative statement. It is the opposite of the "Fuck you" approach or the careless text message. Being diplomatic helps in negotiations where both parties want to understand and be understood, so they are equally motivated towards a solution. Ideally we want this kind of outcome, but sometimes it just doesn't go that way. So it will be of benefit to us to understand why that is.

Courage

Living according to The Good NO requires courage, especially if you have not been able to do it before. Courage is the kind of strength or resolve that drives you to meet a difficult, frightening, painful or disturbing situation head on. This is especially in situations when your resources are challenged or pushed to the limit; when you feel threatened, weak, vulnerable, or intimidated; and when your first instinctive reaction is to run away. At such times, life is throwing an existential question at you. Can you find the courage to stand firm, face your fear and defeat it, or will it defeat you? In the words of the great Nelson Mandela who surely faced fear: 'I learned that courage was not the absence of fear, but the triumph over it. The brave man is not he who does not feel afraid, but he who conquers that fear.'

It takes a lot of courage to live in this world, and to do so in ways that are creative, loving, meaningful and productive. Courage is required in almost every basic human activity or endeavour. For instance, to love and commit to another person takes enormous courage, separating from parents and forging an independent life is a courageous act, and surviving an abusive, traumatic or neglectful relationship with some sense of dignity and with your integrity intact demonstrates tremendous courage and resilience. Career or relationship changes require courage, getting old certainly demands courage, and it takes courage to authentically be yourself in the world, as does wholeheartedly pursuing your dreams.

Courage is the empowering experience of making a decision to stand up and, like Shakespeare's Hamlet (Act III, Scene I), suffer the:

'...slings and arrows of outrageous fortune or to take arms against a sea of troubles and, by opposing, end them.'

Or, when wounded or knocked down to follow Frank Sinatra's advice from his 1962 *Sinatra and Swingin' Brass* album and,

'...pick yourself up, dust yourself off, and start all over again.'

In the final analysis, courage is essentially an existential choice to stand and confront your fears, when appropriate, or to run and hide: to tolerate or challenge rather than cower and withdraw; to persevere rather than quit; to act with integrity rather than expedience; to take responsibility rather than slough it off; to embrace reality rather than retreat; to move forward in your life rather than stagnate or go backwards; to love rather than hate; and to deal with one's demons rather than avoid or deny them.

Chapter 1: The power of the good no

The Good No Formula

The formula for saying NO without feeling guilty is: be honest and concise, and, only if you want to, offer a reason or an explanation. For example: I cannot commit (that's the NO) to that right now because (the reason) I have other priorities (it's brief and vague – don't get bogged down in details).

1. Be brief, direct and non-negotiable. Keep it simple.
2. Don't be wishy-washy or insincere. A weak NO is ineffective.
3. Don't say, 'I'll think about it' if you don't want to do it. This will just prolong the agony and stress you out.
4. Avoid prevaricating by saying things like 'I am not sure' and 'I don't know' and replace that with, 'Let me get back to you on that'.
5. Be assertive and take a stand. Establish eye contact, smile and say a well-modulated NO.
6. Be courteous. A polite 'Thanks for asking' shows you care.
7. Don't lie or apologise unless you are really desperate.
8. Don't be afraid to repeat your NO but avoid the overkill. A hysterical NO is scary.
9. Instead of giving excuses say 'Just because...'
10. It is better to say NO now than to be bitter and resentful later.
11. Practice your good NO. Imagine a scenario and then practice saying NO either by yourself or role play with a friend. This will get you feeling a lot more comfortable with saying it.
12. Develop self-respect. Your self-worth does not depend on how much you do for other people or what they think of you.
13. Integrity is revealed in the response you make in the face of the other person's insistence or badgering. Don't let them get under your skin.

14. Understand other peoples' sneaky tactics and set your boundaries accordingly. This is used when those close to you expect you to do stuff for them just because you are good at it or they think you won't mind. They take it for granted since you've always said Yes before.

Examples of How To Say the Good No

- The plain straight up refuse to argue the point: NO.
- The direct: NO, I can't or NO, I don't want to.
- The polite: NO thank you.
- The taken for granted: NO, I'm not available.
- Leave the door open a crack: NO for now, but maybe later.
- Another version of this is: NO, not now, I will have to think about it.
- The, I do not think the same way as you do: NO, I disagree.
- The just plain I do not care: NO, not interested.
- The diplomatic and formal: NO, it's not possible.
- It's a No to that but a possibility for the other: NO, but...
- The personal policy (used with telemarketers): NO, I do not respond to cold calling.
- Because I can: NO, I have changed my mind.
- Self-discipline, what can I say: NO, I can resist that extra muffin.
- Express regret only if you mean it: NO, I'm sorry I can't go.
- Gratitude goes a long way: Thanks for asking, but NO thanks.
- Used when complaining or giving feedback: I do not like that, so please stop.
- The strong firm: NO, you are invading my privacy or ignoring my rights.
- In desperate circumstances only, you may just have to lie: NO, I can't make it, I tested positive for COVID.

Chapter 1: The power of the good no

SOME MORE FINESSED EXAMPLES OF THE GOOD NO

- Thanks for including me. I appreciate it. Unfortunately, I'm not available.
- Respectfully, it's none of your business.
- I'm not really interested, thanks anyway. You go ahead I'm sure you'll enjoy it.
- Thanks for the invitation but I'm not really up for a kid's birthday party. It's not fun for me.
- NO thanks I'm busy, maybe another time. Keep me in the loop though.
- Thanks for your advice. I will keep that in mind, but I'd rather figure this out for myself.
- The timing isn't great for me, I'll see you another time.
- I can't commit to this as I have other priorities.
- I am in the middle of doing something and now is not a good time.
- I have a long-term commitment that I cannot break.
- Thank you for thinking of me, however, I already made plans.
- I would love to, but I have to say NO.
- My calendar is jam-packed. Can we talk about it next week?

It is reasonable and often necessary to say NO to your family at times. Even though they may cajole and threaten because they want you to do something, they will not be mortally wounded if you do not. Disappointed maybe, but that's not a fatal condition. For instance, if you turn the tables wouldn't you rather they were honest about not wanting to come to your big event, rather than coming and being a pain. No-one should feel guilty for making an honest decision. Families often get caught up in unchanging, age old habits, customs and rituals that originate in the past and get dragged kicking and screaming into the present. These habits are upheld by guilt, manipulation and the fear of change, to name a few. As the years go by you find yourself trapped in the chokehold of obligation, not wanting to rock the boat even though you no longer understand the reason for the ritual. You are scared that if you say NO you might come across as being blunt, insensitive, or thoughtless, and you don't want to be blamed for hurt feelings or looking as though you don't care. However, just remember that it is indeed reasonable and very necessary to say a well-founded NO to your family.

THE GOOD NO IN PRACTICE

Prelude: The decision to introduce a good NO to a situation may mean breaking years of habit, tradition and avoidance. So you need to prepare yourself. It's difficult making these decisions when you have a long-standing avoidance of saying NO. Being afraid to stand up for yourself is a common problem. So it's important to think the situation over before giving a response, but not too much thinking. If you overthink something you can send yourself into a repetitive loop of 'should I' or 'shouldn't I'. Saying NO is a decision that weighs heavily on the decision maker who now has to act, and that means following through.

First step: Consider the request being made of you, listen and don't interrupt. Allow yourself a space to think. Keep things simple and clear without over-explaining. Use a cordial tone of voice; be polite and respectful. In the beginning, it's about rallying your resolve and summoning your courage. Once you get going you will find relief at being able to conduct yourself with openness and honesty.

Second step: Back yourself up. Keep in mind that learning to say NO is a skill that takes time, effort, and practice to develop. You have legitimate reasons to say NO to things and to people, particularly when it requires you to do something that's unreasonable, inconsiderate, or inconvenient, or that takes you away from your own priorities. Saying NO isn't easy if

Chapter 1: The power of the good no

you're inclined to say Yes all the time. However, learning to say NO is a vital part of simplifying your life and staying away from situations that can create unnecessary stress. With practice, saying NO gets easier and easier.

Third step: Manage your fear. If the thought of saying NO makes you anxious then perhaps you need to think about ways that you can better manage your fear or anxiety. You will need to address the cause of it and then how it is manifested in your body. The effects in your body can be addressed by being mindful of your breathing to start with, and the cause of your anxiety may require some reflection or a therapeutic response.

Fourth step: Follow up. Establishing a meditation practice can help to maintain a balanced attention between the mind and the breath. Reflect on situations where you would like to say NO, but are too scared to say anything. Now scan your body for any signs of stress or discomfort and breathe deeply into those areas. Take care to inflate your lungs fully and keep your breath even and calm. Use this technique to deal with stressful emotions before moving onto verbalising how you feel. Start small and build up to more difficult situations.

Remember, never take the name of The Good NO as a justification to withhold from someone or be rejecting by denying him or her, just for the hell of it. It is not a means for you to act out or to perversely punish another person. Nor should you use it to avoid your responsibilities or to cop out. The Good NO is intended to be used with integrity. Do not take it lightly.

Applying NO more often will lead to your living a better, less stressful life. The ability to say NO means relegating the space to be able to do those things you need to do, like going to work, taking the kids to school, catching up with friends, studying for an exam, doing your tax return and so forth.

Then there are the bigger things you might want to do that require a commitment, like taking on a course of study, writing a book, travelling, joining a committee or a book club and so much more. Saying NO is a relief, it means less time wasted and more time focusing on what you need and want to do. Saying NO helps you to stick to your values and set boundaries for your Yes's to take shape. NO is a short simple word but for some people it's extremely difficult to say.

▶▶▶

Chapter 2:
What interferes with The Good No?

Smile and the world smiles with you, cry and you cry alone.
                    Stanley Gordon West in *Growing An Inch*

The list of things that interfere with saying the good NO is extremely long. Saying NO doesn't mean that you are a bad person nor does it mean you are being rude, selfish, or unkind. These are all unhelpful mind-sets that make it hard to say NO. Having the self-knowledge to understand where certain beliefs come from is a great way to learn how to let go of them. Did you ever wonder why it was so easy to say NO when you were little and why it has become so much harder as you age? What's happened to us over the years? Babies and young children are great at refusing to do what they don't want to do; they spit their food out, throw tantrums, walk away when you're talking to them, won't wear what you want them to, scream when they feel like it and so on. As they get older children are taught to be socially appropriate. This means that saying NO becomes impolite or wrong. If you said NO to your parents, your teacher, your uncle or your grandparents you were most certainly considered rude, and you would probably have been reprimanded for it, punished even. You are shown that saying NO is off limits, and you learn that saying Yes is the polite, likable and fake thing to do. As children we are controlled by an adult world and we follow their lead. Some parents want their children to conform to their views and obey their directives without instructing them on how to think and decide for themselves. We human beings hold onto our childhood beliefs rather tightly and we continue to associate NO with being unlikeable, bad mannered, egotistical or mean. We worry that if we say NO we will feel guilty and ashamed, and wind up alone and abandoned with no friends. These are powerful misconceptions that keep us saying Yes.

One of the most noticeable features of the human psyche is how little we understand it. Although you live with yourself day in and day out, you rarely manage to make sense of more than a fraction of who you really are. Your self-ignorance regularly surprises and troubles you, but you brush it away because you don't know what to do about it. For example, for no apparent reason you may feel angry towards someone you thought you loved, or you might be more jealous than nice people ought to be. You feel things without knowing why and experience a basic division between two areas of your mind - the conscious and the unconscious parts i.e. what's immediately accessible to you and what is unknown and lies beneath your awareness. A lot of what is unconscious is complicated material that we are unable to look at too closely. Unwanted material is blocked from awareness by repression as a mechanism of defence to protect the ego or self. Sigmund Freud believed that the unconscious continues to influence our behaviour even though we are unaware of its underlying influences. We are often unaware or unconscious of many of the factors that determine our emotions, thoughts and actions. These unconscious dynamics may be the source of considerable distress and suffering for some of us, in the form of symptoms or as troubling personality traits, difficulties in work or in love relationships, or disturbances in mood. A psychoanalytic approach can reveal how unconscious beliefs affect current relationships and patterns of behaviour, trace them back to their origins, show how they have developed over time, and help the individual to understand the meaning of this and to deal better with the realities of adult life.

Chapter 2: What interferes with The Good No?

People often prefer the ease of not knowing and preserving the status quo in preference to the changes we know we ought to make in our day-to-day life. We go through life in a preordained way doing things out of habit and in response to whims and trends. Blindly we keep moving towards something that we are not certain is our goal because it was originally someone else's. A lack of knowledge is what most interferes with the good NO and self-knowledge is necessary to gain access to what you really want in life.

Fear

I must not fear. Fear is the mind-killer. Fear is the little death that brings total obliteration. I will face my fear. I will permit it to pass over me and through me. And when it has gone past, I will turn the inner eye to see its path. Where the fear has gone, there will be nothing. Only I will remain.

Dune by Frank Herbert

One of the greatest obstacles to experiencing the good NO is fear, in particular not knowing why you are afraid. Fear is your instinctive response to a perceived threat that leaves you on full alert as you anticipate a real or, more often, imagined danger. Things that cause us fear are around us all the time and if we give way to all of them we would never get out of bed. We fear the other person's response to us, we fear change or having to do something differently, we fear new experiences, we fear being seen and not being seen, we fear the unknown and the list of our fears goes on forever. We are thinking beings and consequently we fear. It often manifest in thoughts like: What will they think of me? I don't want to appear rude. If I say NO they won't like me. What if they don't believe me? etc.

The more we indulge this kind of fear-based mindset the more afraid we become. Facing our fears requires integrity, conviction and true grit.

Fear and its synonyms anxiety, dread, terror, distress, apprehension, alarm, fright, panic, and trepidation are emotions and like all emotions they send you messages that you interpret based on how you perceive the environment around you. Fear can be one of the more difficult emotions to decipher, especially when you first take on a challenge. Fear really tests a person and like a muscle your response to fear can be strengthened. Every time you make a change it forces you to grow in some way because you are stepping outside your comfort zone. By definition, being outside of your comfort zone will make you feel some discomfort that is a prerequisite for growth. You will need to investigate your thinking around your fear and be brave enough to consciously put yourself in the position to face your fears. But you know that the sooner you learn to stop procrastinating and avoiding, the easier it will be to harness that bravery. Just do it before you have any time to think about it. Avoid the torturous loop of

Chapter 2: What interferes with The Good No?

questions and considerations of all the options. Just do it. This is short-term pain for long-term gain.

Feel the fear and do it anyway, is a pearl of wisdom from Susan Jeffers who also said that underlying all our fears is a lack of trust in ourselves. The message is 'don't fight your fear, feel it and move towards it courageously'. Courage is not the absence of fear; it is feeling the fear and facing it head on. Fear is an opportunity for you to grow into someone you respect. Fearfulness or cowardice, on the other hand, occurs when your fear gets in the way of you taking a risk, any risk. It is the opposite of courage and indicates how you might be letting yourself down in the face of a challenge. Cowardice means hiding behind someone else and allowing him or her to take the fall for something you did or when you hurt someone else to protect yourself. A coward evades responsibility so they never experience the consequences of their actions. They develop strategies over time to avoid stepping up when needed, they fake being confident and they rarely take positive action. It's okay to feel vulnerable and want to protect yourself when you're scared, that's normal. Some compassion around this is helpful. But you will need to come out of hiding to own up to your mistakes and be fair to yourself and others.

Overcoming a fear of rejection by saying NO is essentially you taking control of your life. Rather than feeling trapped, resentful or guilty making your intentions clear helps you grow a sense of freedom and empowerment instead. All this requires motivation, you need to want things to be different and you need to find the reason for this by yourself. The Hebrew word chutzpah depicts a kind of attitude that there is nothing stopping you from doing whatever you want. Chutzpah is, for the most part, audacity but it also has a mix of insolence, impudence, boldness, cheek, willpower, and arrogance. It's the kind of confidence needed to face your fear and speak your good NO.

FOMO

Fear Of Missing Out or FOMO are people who cannot stand missing out on potential rewards like fun, adventure, love, special events etc. They are ruled by regret about what they might have missed out on and are always over-committed and over-involved because they have to be included in everything. They want what the other person has. FOMO people have way too many expectations of themselves and others. They are filled with concern that something may happen that they will miss out on so their response is always, 'Yes, count me in'. They need to try a discerning NO from time to time.

Then there is the Fear Of Having No Friends or FOHNF group. You will do anything to avoid being alone. You are frightened of being by yourself because it produces awareness of the emptiness inside, something we all have encountered at some point. Rather than sit alone with the angst and wait for it to pass you run to others for support. These poor FOHNF's desperately need people around them; any people, even toxic people. You endure rudeness, insensitivity, drunkenness and aggression without comment or complaint. You will marry the wrong person for fear of being left on the shelf. You sacrifice your principles in order to be included, and in the process bankrupt yourself. After a while you no longer recognise who you are because you have compromised yourself so much. FOHNF people need to speak the good NO because it represents a stand-alone decision; it defines the individual in that moment. That NO expresses a position and that position has an impact.

THE TYRANNY OF NICENESS

Nice people don't typically like to see other people upset or cause upset to them. Being too nice or shouldering problems and emotions that are not yours to carry is a quick way to being swamped with an

Chapter 2: What interferes with The Good No?

unmanageable amount of real-life responsibilities. You will be volunteered for activities without anyone consulting you first or accepting more than your fair share of work because it is assumed that you'll agree to it, and you are too nice to refuse. You just go along with it because by now you have rationalised that it is acceptable to be taken advantage of. Most women have a difficult time saying NO, especially if they think someone's feelings may be at stake or if they think they won't be liked. There is nothing wrong with being liked but women are socialised to be in-tune emotionally with others. This is actually a socially learned coping mechanism that can, with a little time and attention, be unlearned. Boys, on the other hand, are stereotyped as being less in-tune with people's feelings. What this means is that when heterosexual girls and boys, and women and men start playing together, women are at somewhat of a disadvantage. They want to play nice, whereas the guys just want to win – at least that's how the stereotype goes. There is something wrong when girls and women learn to subvert their own needs to the point that they are taken advantage of or end up doing things they don't want to do.

The tyranny of niceness is operated by a mechanism that regulates a perimeter that is somehow switched off. Priority is paid to obeying the dictates of niceness in such a way that you cannot defend your own honour. Worse still is that we idealise the nice person by saying: 'Jim is such a nice guy he will do anything for you' or 'sheila is so nice I never hear her say a bad word against anyone'. It's nice to be thought of as nice but being pigeonholed this way can be like a straight jacket that shuts you up.

Toxic positivity

Toxic positivity is the belief that no matter how dire or difficult a situation might be people should maintain a positive mindset – let's look on the bright side, 'zip-a-dee-doo-dah' approach to life. While being optimistic and engaging in positive thinking has its benefits, toxic positivity rejects difficult emotions in favour of a falsely positive, cheerful facade that denies reality. Life isn't always positive and we humans all have to deal with painful emotions and experiences that, while unpleasant and hard to deal with, are important and need to be felt and experienced with openness and honesty.

Toxic positivity can take a wide variety of forms, some you may have encountered and some you may have perpetrated:

- In a crisis, such as losing a job, you tell yourself 'just stay positive' or 'look on the bright side.' Such thoughts produce fear and tend to be a way of shutting you down.
- After experiencing a loss, such as the death of a family member you say, 'Everything happens for a reason.' This statement avoids the pain of your loss and communicates to those around you that if they speak of their loss it's just another sob story. If that's so, keep your mouth shut and don't say anything.
- A person expresses disappointment or sadness and you say 'Happiness is a choice' or 'You'll get over it'. Your response suggests blame regarding negative emotions. While we are all responsible for our choices your trite platitudes let you off the hook so you don't have to deal with other people's feelings. If you don't know what else to say and don't know how to be empathetic, again, just be quiet.

Toxic positivity denies people the authentic support they need firstly as a common courtesy, secondly as a sign of respect for their feelings and thirdly to help them cope with what they are facing. It leaves them feeling dismissed, ignored and invalidated. When someone is suffering, they need to know that their emotions are valid, and that

Chapter 2: What interferes with The Good No?

they can get some relief talking to friends and family, and a friendly shoulder to cry on. Toxic positivity sends a message that if you aren't finding a way to feel positive, even in the face of tragedy, then you are doing something wrong. It functions as an avoidance mechanism for uncomfortable feelings that get dismissed and denied. The avoidance of painful emotions denies the person the ability to face challenging feelings that can ultimately lead to growth and deeper insight.

Toxic positivity is seen in situations where a problem or crisis is ignored and dismissed, rather than the emergency being faced and doing what needs to be done. People cover the problem up, dumb it down and deny the importance of dealing with it. This is often seen in groups such as parliamentary workplaces, as mentioned earlier, where no one stands up against passive aggression or bullying to say 'something is really wrong with this'. They duck their heads down pretending not to notice what has happened. They avoid facing reality, feeling their feelings and taking social responsibility. The consequence of this kind of behaviour is that it catches on in the workplace culture and before you know it everyone is afraid to have an opinion or speak up. Say if some of these people have come from a background of abuse or violence then their responses to this kind of workplace will be heightened. When something dramatic happens they are frozen like rabbits in the headlights. The environment becomes risk averse and everything is dumbed down or has a positive spin on it to avoid any drama, thus denying the reality that 'shit happens'. Acknowledging the seriousness of a situation allows it to be seen realistically and managed appropriately.

If you've been affected by toxic positivity or if you recognise this kind of behaviour in yourself, there are things that you can do to take a healthier, more supportive approach. Some ideas are:

- Recognise and manage your own negative emotions, rather than denying them.
- Be realistic about what you ought to feel. It's normal to feel stressed, worried, or even fearful when you are facing a difficult situation.
- It's okay to feel more than one thing at a time. Your emotions are as complex as the situation itself.
- Focus on listening to others and showing support. When someone expresses a difficult emotion, let them know that what they are feeling is valid and that you are there to listen to them. Do not shut them down.
- Notice how you feel. Instead of automatically avoiding difficult emotions, give yourself permission to feel them and identify them. It may feel challenging at first but you'll get used to it. These feelings are real, valid, and important. They can provide you with information about yourself and help you to see things about a situation that you might need to work on or change.
- Emotions need to be symbolised with words otherwise you get stuck with unprocessed feelings and you will be unaware of where they have come from. Speak with someone who cares and who will listen respectfully.

So when you are going through hard times, think about ways you can give voice to your emotions in a manner that's productive rather than unrealistically positive. Research suggests that just putting what you are feeling into words can help lower the intensity of negative feelings. The happiness industry posits that we all deserve to be happy and free from suffering. But human experience is grounded in suffering and how we do or do not deal with it is important. Toxic positivity produces pseudo success; it is based on ignorance of the reality of life and refusal to see that there is also a negative side that we have to tolerate being aware of. If you need help talk to someone wise you can trust.

Chapter 2: What interferes with The Good No?

NICE GIRL SYNDROME

Within the nice girl (yes it's most often girls but not always) syndrome are some deeply rooted feelings of not being good enough. The self-image of a miss goody-two-shoes is constructed around the idea that you have to be nice in order to be loved and accepted. Both nice girls and good girls are programmed not to hurt other people's feelings. You have an overinflated sense of your capacity to hurt others based on your own fragile self-image. This is the projection of your own feelings and intentions onto someone else and that's why you are so scared of saying the wrong thing. You avoid disagreeing with others or giving strong opinions because that would spoil the veneer of niceness. If you are a nice girl, you are the thoughtful one at work who remembers to buy a gift for the person who is leaving and it's you who cleans up the tearoom. You are the do-gooder who volunteers for everything and will do overtime for no extra pay even if it inconveniences you. When you feel sad or angry you smile. You have learned from an early age that smiling makes the world smile back. Which is kind of true but smiling even when you feel like crying is a bit absurd, don't you think?

Maintaining a façade of the nice girl does not allow you to see or accept your own darker side. You cannot receive feedback or criticism without it being taken personally. This is because criticism is perceived as an act of injustice and feels like a threat. You make all these efforts to be good and nice and perfect and still it's not enough! Admitting that you can sometimes be less than perfect makes you churn up inside and you deny it all. When someone tells you something that remotely implies you are deficient you go into fight or flight mode. You desperately have to protect that image.

If you put all your energy into being nice and good you end up not representing yourself honestly. No one is that nice or that good all the time; it's not possible for a human being. Your voice becomes more passive and, in each encounter, you come out the victim. Thus, you are unable to trust anyone or sustain healthy boundaries. Being chronically insecure and scared of displeasing others tends to progress over time leaving you with feelings of shame and guilt because all your efforts have not been good enough. You can't make decisions, manage your time properly or accomplish goals, and high levels of anxiety arise resulting in burnout. This form of cowardice leads you to misery and suffering. Ultimately, it is you who has to decide. Where is your self-respect?

Stop smiling all the time unless you are truly happy or at least a bit pleased about something. Remember to cry when you are sad or hurt, let the tears flow and laugh when you are happy. Learn to develop emotional flexibility again like you did as a child. Start looking more honestly at your so-called negative traits. The good, the bad and the ugly are all parts of you, besides they have been leaking out for ages, but you have been blind to it. Accept and embrace that you might be a bit passive aggressive sometimes. You see that wasn't so hard. It's a scary process learning to be aware of yourself and, admittedly it can be a bit painful, but self-knowledge will not kill you.

Chapter 2: What interferes with The Good No?

A serious issue for nice girls is the attraction to the wrong kind of man. He is either married, 35 years older than you, is a pervert, has some type of addiction, and is a criminal, or worse, a sociopath. Basically, you choose men who are unavailable; they will never fully commit to a relationship but you hang in there for as long as there is something to fight for. You think he will change or that you can make him into a better man; good luck with that. You hold on for grim death to hide your fear and, in the end, you can blame it all on him. The only way to manage nice girl syndrome is to be aware of the patterns you keep repeating and understand why you do it. Once you start to appreciate yourself more you will be wiser about your fascination with the wrong man.

A simple yet punchy message in the lyrics of Meghan Trainor's 2016 song 'NO' inspire women to let go and say No. Look it up on YouTube. It goes like this:

> All my ladies listen up
> If that boy ain't giving up
> Lick your lips and swing your hips
> Girl all you gotta say is
>
> My name is no
> My sign is no
> My number is no
> You need to let it go
> You need to let it go
> Need to let it go
> Nah to the ah to the, no, no, no....

THE SOFT TOUCH

Being nice is often about avoiding conflict, letting inappropriate actions slide, or bottling up words

and actions that ought to be spoken and enacted to prevent creating an uncomfortable scene. At its worst, being nice reinforces actions and attitudes that strip away human dignity.

- Bruce Reyes-Chow

A kind, nice person who does not have firm boundaries is often passive and will probably be taken advantage of in some way sooner or later. That is not to suggest that you should stop being nice, it's just that you have to know when it's time to close the door on negative situations that might cause you harm. Human beings should be seen for the paradoxes they are – kind and cruel, compassionate and cold, charitable and selfish. The timeworn idiom from Yorkshire in England, 'There's nowt so queer as folk' means that some people's behaviour can be tricky, peculiar or strange. The complex nature of people is well known, as is the ability to survive and thrive in this world by balancing the multiple facets of the human experience. Remember that most people are complicated in one way or another, even you.

Chapter 2: What interferes with The Good No?

It's not unusual for people to view unwarranted niceness with suspicion. Unexpected niceness can pique a sense of danger in someone who is not anticipating it. They can't identify what your intentions are and wonder if you might take advantage of them or have an ulterior motive for being kind. Be aware that you could encounter this type of response when you are indiscriminately nice. Predators and users tend to shy away from people who don't allow themselves to be manipulated. It's good to surround yourself with civilised people, but it's just as important not to lose sight of the difficult self-absorbed nature of humanity. Being too nice will leave you vulnerable and could be a hindrance in competitive environments, like the workplace and business, particularly if you make the mistake of expecting that the person opposite you will be nice and treat you with the same respect. People looking for an edge will hone in on a nice person assuming they are 'a soft touch' or a pushover. Others will test the boundaries of nice people; they will push to see just how much they can get away with. If you do push back they will try to retract their behaviour by telling you it was a misunderstanding, you took them the wrong way, or they were just joking.

It's a common manipulative ploy that tells you a lot about the person you're dealing with. People like this are typically looking for weaknesses in your boundaries, which they will find sooner or later if you let them continue poking around because you are too nice to say NO. In many cases, you'll find that people like this had their niceness taken advantage of at some earlier point in time.

The types of person who will exploit a nice kind person just don't care about your feelings or respect your time or your responsibilities. They couldn't care less! Have you heard of the saying about 'A wolf in sheep's clothing?' This is someone who will take advantage of your niceness by masquerading as a nice person when really they are playing the role of a double agent. They pretend to be nice and friendly so they can get close to you and then take advantage of the situation; they are really quite dangerous and very tricky people. Sociopathic comes to mind.

This vignette identifies Clara who thought that the handsome stranger was gentle and kind, the nicest man she'd met in a long time. He was someone she could take home to meet her parents. But her friend Alan suspected he was a wolf in sheep's clothing, and told Clara that the stranger was too good to be true. He couldn't understand how Clara was unable to tell that there was something not quite right about this guy. Alan is suspicious of strangers, but Clara takes everyone at face value. Who do you think is right – Alan or Clara? What do you think about nice people who are too good to be true?

There are times when it is good or necessary to provide additional justification to a NO, particularly if you're trying to find a middle ground with someone. Beware that justification offers a manipulative person a potential in-road to inject self-doubt and undermine your good NO. This is because people who are both nice and naive often want to see the best in other people.

Predators like narcissists, manipulators, and users target nice people because they are often easy to steamroll, manipulate, don't ask the right questions, don't establish boundaries or enforce them, and have a hard

Chapter 2: What interferes with The Good No?

time watching other people suffer. A commonly used manipulative technique is to paint oneself as a victim in a hard cruel world, of course leaving out their role in it all. Sob stories like the following are typical:

'They had it in for me from the start.'
'All of my ex-partners were crazy.'
'I never get any support from anyone.'
'No one understands me like you do.'
'It wasn't my fault.'

A naive person who does not question the motives or inconsistencies in this kind of manipulative ploy will be sucked in. It's not too cynical to say that if you are completely unquestioning you put yourself in the position of being manipulated. The simplest way to counteract this is to wake up. Start thinking for yourself; pay attention, listen for inconsistencies and question the motives of others. You can sympathise with another person's story but don't let your emotions cloud your judgment.

Here is the example of George who sent money online to a young man from Fiji. He had met this guy whilst on a trip to Fiji some five years earlier and they had kept in touch via Facebook. Out of a sense of kindness and sympathy George sent money to him last year because of the COVID situation there. Later in another message, this guy talked about being poor and George felt obliged to send more money. Within a month there was another request for more money. George is on a pension and smokes cigarettes, which means he is poor too. But George is a nice guy; he likes to please people and has a hard time saying NO. He turned himself inside out in an effort to raise money for the guy in Fiji by starting up a Facebook campaign. He found himself begging for money from friends and acquaintances, and this left him feeling ashamed and anxious. He was caught in a web of his own making but eventually he was brave enough to confess this to the guy in Fiji who was aghast. He assumed that George had plenty of money and was simply being generous. They came to an understanding.

PEOPLE PLEASERS

There are lots of reasons why yes sayers, fence sitters, and people pleasers say Yes to unacceptable requests based on their desire to please others. Feeling as though you should or ought to say Yes to people so as to appease them or for them to like you is like living in an internal dictatorship. Being too nice for your own good, you tend to agree to things you're not interested in and do favours for everyone even though you do not have the time. Being a good person is often interpreted as you being helpful, agreeable, and generally a good team player. People pleasers don't want to disappoint or offend others, they feel obliged, don't want to be rude, and feel guilty if they refuse. They pacify and appease, always saying Yes to friends, family and anyone who is in need. People pleasers, fence sitters and 'Yes' people are so nice that they feel as though they have been backed into a corner and have no choice. They are Yes addicts and at the mercy of their inability to say No. They may have principles but they do not represent them.

People pleasers are not just nice people who try to make everyone happy. They suffer from, what Harriet Braiker calls, *the Disease to Please* where they say Yes when they really want to say No but can't. They feel the need for approval of others like an addictive pull. Their debilitating fear of expressing anger and confrontation force them to use people pleasing as camouflage. They may appear to the outside world as regular nice people, but they are concealing the nature of their anger and resentment behind a public happy face. This may start innocently enough with genuine attempts to make others happy. However, this seemingly harmless passion to put others first and to compulsively please them, even at the expense of their own health and happiness, rapidly spirals

Chapter 2: What interferes with The Good No?

into a serious psychological syndrome with far-reaching physical and emotional consequences. The disease to please reveals the underlying addiction to approval. Unhealthy mindsets fuel the fear and emotional avoidance patterns that perpetuate the problem including the avoidance of anger and rejection. This need for approval usually originates from the child's relationship with their parents or caregivers. As discussed previously, people-pleasing patterns are deeply ingrained and associated with parental acceptance. Early programming of adaptation is perceived as intimately tied to survival in a family. These patterns are established in childhood and like any addiction are very tough to influence or change. In fact, people pleasers are only ready to alter their ways when their lives have started to feel unmanageable, out of control or are falling apart.

Imagine this: You had planned a catch up with an old friend, but your mother has requested you visit her instead because she is lonely. You fear the consequences of saying No to her. Your friend will be disappointed and you will too because that's what you really wanted to do. But your mum makes you feel guilty if you say No to her; remember there's a long history between the two of you. She says, 'It's okay I don't mind if you can't make it, I'll just sit here by myself. I'm used to it. No one ever visits me. I could die and they wouldn't find my body for days.' This is emotional manipulation and is as old as the hills. You are essentially caught between a rock and a hard place. It takes a lot of time and work to negotiate a path through this one.

The consequence of people pleasing is that you become a pushover for others to manipulate and make use of you. Pushovers are avoidant of conflict and take the path of least resistance. They are unable to refuse anyone, including telemarketers, children and small animals. Thus, people pleasers become unreliable because they are constantly juggling demands by dropping this one to satisfy the other. Low on self-discipline or will power they are indecisive and tend to go with the flow; they never push back and always acquiesce to requests for favours. Having the compulsion to say Yes all the time can be very problematic, especially when it involves sex. What about repeatedly not using condoms because he doesn't like it yet you have been treated for STD's (Sexually Transmitted Disease) three times now. Those who are always giving in to the demands of others deny their own needs and wind up feeling ashamed, unworthy, self-critical and generally not good enough. It's an ever-diminishing circuit, the more you say Yes the less No's you have in you.

Take responsibility for yourself but do not indulge in self-imposed guilt; it is unreasonable and it is irrational. Are you worried about what others will think if you, say No? Get over it; generally they won't even care or will recover faster than you think. If they don't and you get punished for saying No then there are a few home truths you need to face about that person. They are not very nice! Anyone who has to be in control of or dominate another person is probably a bully. Why do you feel guilty when you say No? If you have done something you regret you might want to make up for it by saying Yes when you don't want to. This gives the other person an edge whereby they can apply pressure through that guilt to manipulate you. They are not playing fair. Those closest to you are usually the best at inducing guilt in you. They hint, harass, nag and pester until you give in, they guilt you into saying Yes. You are allowing them to control you. Get a grip on yourself, send out an SOS and call for back up. Decide how you can represent yourself better in these situations in future.

Don't rock the boat

People pleasers are usually brought up in households where love, attention, and affection were obtained inconsistently. They likely had caregivers who were preoccupied with their own big feelings, were too worried or sad or angry to tune into what their children might be thinking and feeling. In many cases, the parents' feelings might even spill over onto the

Chapter 2: What interferes with The Good No?

children, as seen when the parents talk to their children as confidantes and friends, rather than keeping a clear parent/child boundary. So, the children get really good at earning approval from their parents. They do their darndest to have it be a good day for the other person, originally the mother. This is achieved by trying to be pleasing and kind and good to everyone by avoiding any conflict - if everyone else is happy, then they are happy. Maintaining this kind of impossible balance is extremely stressful for a child.

People pleasers are so preoccupied with what others think, want and feel that they are blind to their own needs and feelings. They will even compromise their own principles and integrity if it means keeping a connection going. They do this by not rocking the boat. This means that they pretend certain things aren't such a big deal when they really are. They want to appear easy going so will not make a fuss; they don't want to appear negative or overly sensitive. This avoidance of complaining or saying No in opposition to everyone else who goes along with it is an ingrained societal norm.

For example, Phil is planning to drive home while under the influence of alcohol. You want to object but notice that no one else is saying anything.

You stay silent not rocking that boat, as usual. But Andrew does step forward; he says that it's not okay to allow Phil to drive home in his current condition as he is definitely over the limit. Immediately the room erupts with, 'Leave Phil to make his own decisions', 'Keep out of it, don't interfere', 'He's a grown man, he can take care of himself' and the best of all 'He hasn't had that much to drink'. The group closes ranks denying the reality of what is patently obvious, and colluding with their collective dishonesty. This is classic gaslighting where the veracity of what Andrew has observed is questioned in such a way that it shuts him down and he starts to question what he has observed. But Andrew is made of sterner stuff and so are you. Your job is to recognise what is happening in scenarios like this, to know that this kind of behaviour is not okay and what you can do about it. First you need to find your voice and back Andrew up.

Too good to be true

What happens when the nice people pleasing person is pouring too much of themselves into another person without getting anything back in return. Friendships and relationships are supposed to be reciprocal and mutually beneficial in some way, aren't they? You can't constantly pour niceness and kindness into others without it eventually depleting your resources. We all need some encouragement to keep on giving, even if it's only breadcrumbs. That process of depletion gets much quicker if the person is a close friend or significant other who is not giving anything back to you. Inevitably, resentment builds and the relationship starts to form cracks and then big gaping chasms appear. Giving too much without anything coming back in return is a warning sign to stop giving so much and stop being so nice and pleasing. It's time to take stock, don't you think?

What nice people tend to do is internalise or hold onto fears and negative emotions that naturally rise up in the course of everyday life. We all go through positive and negative circumstances because life is like that; it's random, changeable and certainly can get chaotic at times. Some people devote too much time and energy on being nice to other people as a form of self-medicating and avoid confronting their own problems or addressing their own needs. This is a waste of time because one day you will look around and see that years have passed by without any meaningful progress being made on how to alleviate your own suffering or find some peace of mind. Understandably, the by-product of this can be misery and angst.

It's also manifested in impulsive behaviour and acting out in ways such as, one-night stands, criminal activity, binge drinking or drug taking, throwing a tantrum or directing rage at an innocent bystander. Stress and pressure build up until finally apparently insignificant triggers can set you off. Being nice is all well and good but never forget to treat yourself just as nicely as you treat others before it's too late.

Niceness and amiability are qualities that this world is in dire need of, but life is about balance. There are times when being nice is not the best thing, particularly when it comes to preserving the sanctity of your personal space, peace of mind, and happiness. Many good people do not want to be perceived as mean, rude, or unkind, so they accept being treated poorly or without consideration so as to not cause a disturbance. But you good people must start communicating to the other people around you about what your needs and expectations are. You need to stand up and assert yourselves. Sometimes you have to cause a disturbance if it means being treated with respect. NO is a complete sentence designed for good, nice, kind, people pleasers to take on board.

Altruism and Self-sacrifice

The profound benefits of altruism in our modern society are self-evident. Altruism is the ability to experience compassion and relatively conflict free pleasure from contributing to the welfare of others, as distinguished from the need to sacrifice oneself for the benefit of others. Again the question is one of self-understanding and balancing of priorities. Altruism and self-sacrifice or masochism often coexist and intermingle making it hard to be clear about what is what so it's worth delving into this a little. Gaining knowledge and understanding about various aspects of human behaviour only increases our ability to make decisions that are in line with what we really want rather than on self-deception.

A masochist derives some form of gratification through self-sacrifice and suffering. The enjoyment a person experiences in suffering can be addictive and is habitually denied by the individual. This masochistic enjoyment is reminiscent of a concept called jouissance introduced by the French psychoanalyst Jacques Lacan. Jouissance is a French word that cannot be precisely translated but is related to the verb jouir, referring to an enjoyment that's excessive or beyond pleasure. Yet according to Lacan in his book on ethics, the result of transgressing the pleasure principle is not more pleasure but pain, since there is only a certain amount of pleasure that someone can bear. Beyond this limit, pleasure becomes pain, and this 'painful principle' is what Lacan called jouissance. Thus, jouissance is the satisfaction you derive from your own suffering, and that suffering can be addictive.

What we value in the altruistic good side of human nature, can also have a dark side. Some of us, who have been socialised by coercive gender norms, can be particularly self-sacrificing. This is generally because something was disturbed in primary childhood identifications. Empathic feelings for others, coupled with a desire to be liked, the narrow-minded feelings of those around you, emotional contagion, motivated reasoning, selective exposure, and even an egocentric belief

Chapter 2: What interferes with The Good No?

that you know what is best for others, can lead to powerful and often irrational misconceptions about what helping actually is. Apparent good intentions can blind people to the detrimental consequences of their actions. In more primitive and unhealthy forms of what looks like altruism, the individual projects their own desires onto the other person as a narcissistic extension of themselves. This is done in order to satisfy their own needs, often mistakenly deeming their motivation as altruistic because it looks and sounds better. However, those capable of genuine altruism recognise and respect the autonomous wishes of the person they are contributing to and enjoy enhancing their success rather than developing a co-dependency. Across human history there are many examples of the questionable motives and the unintended negative consequences of apparent altruism on the self and others. This dynamic of pathological altruism involves subjectively pro-social acts that are objectively antisocial.

The research of Barbara Oakley and her colleagues suggest that many harmful activities from co-dependency to martyrdom and suicide are committed with the stated altruistic intention of helping others. Instances of well intentioned, albeit misguided, actions that go very wrong are: an animal lover who lives with 25 cats in their one bedroom flat, compulsive giving until there is nothing left to live on, guilt-giving to assuage a perceived crime, volunteering for ideological reasons to participate in risky ventures, Christian missionaries who went forth all over the world to convert the natives to the gospel of god, and then there is the example of the stolen generation with the practice of removing indigenous children from their families to be raised in religious institutions in the misguided belief that it was for their own good. In essence, pathological or unhealthy altruism might actually be thought of as any personal tendency that promotes the welfare of another, but instead of beneficial outcomes, this altruism has irrational and substantial negative consequences to both the other person and to themselves.

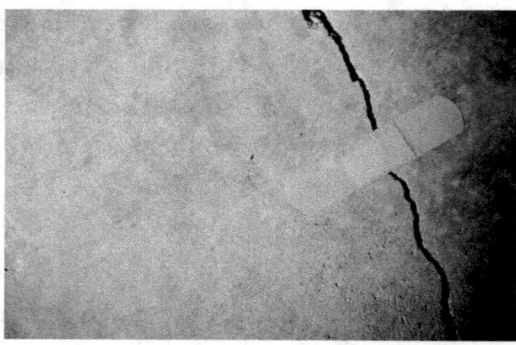

Signs of self-punishment or masochism in someone is seen in the form of the following:

1. You can't say NO. The number one sign that someone is a masochist is that they are unable to say NO. If you're not sure whether to say Yes or No, pause and take a breather. Does your inclination to say Yes come from a desire to please someone or seek approval? Saying NO is not selfish or unkind—it's an act of self-care. Check your motivations and give yourself permission to refuse.

2. You're extremely invested in looking good. You're religious about your morning routine. You walk every day, even when you're sick, and if you miss it, you feel awful. You won't let yourself cheat on your diet, even when it's your birthday. You beat yourself up when you have too much to drink, and gaining a few pounds turns you into a self-berating exercise tyrant. Ease up. Say NO. While there's nothing wrong with discipline and good intentions, our quirks, eccentricities, triumphs, and mistakes are what make us so delightfully human.

3. You get off on rescuing everyone - people, animals, and the planet. The victim, the martyr, and the perpetrator are three roles in an unhealthy psychological cycle that people often feed into. The only way to unfasten from this pattern is to opt out of it. Check your

Chapter 2: What interferes with The Good No?

motivations any time you're called on for a favour. If you're driven by feelings of unworthiness that lead you to overcompensate, or by a fear of disappointing someone, go inward. Take a breath. Say NO. Soothe the part of you that yearns to rescue, and rescue yourself instead.

4. You resist receiving anything because you believe you don't deserve it. Let others in and allow them to give to you. Develop the practice of acceptance. Just like biceps, your receiving muscles need exercise. Treat yourself to something nice that you do not usually allow.

5. You are attracted to narcissists. Ho hum! Narcissists can be charismatic, compelling, magnetic, and hard to avoid. But if you keep walking straight into them, you're definitely a masochist. Break the pattern now, and spare yourself the heartbreak and disappointment. See the section on narcissists and control freaks.

6. You do not stand up for yourself. It's one thing to be kind, compassionate, and accommodating, but another thing to allow yourself be used as a doormat. Put yourself forward and assert your own needs. It's possible to be multifaceted and embrace all sides of yourself, and that includes a side that won't be taken advantage of.

7. You are perfectionistic. You fear being perceived by others as imperfect. Accept your flaws and the flaws of others. Let it go, they don't really care.

8. You judge yourself for negative emotions. There's no way to avoid feeling sad, lost, disappointed, scared, or angry at times. That's because you're human. While it may help you avoid painful emotions in the short term, suppressing yourself is a soul-destroying sort of masochism. Try to feel what you feel without holding back or judging any emotion as 'wrong.'

9. You're attracted to drama. Drama queens are at the heart of masochism. Give yourself permission to prioritise the people and situations

that cultivate the stillness in you.

10. You reject anything that feels too good. The inability to relax into simple pleasures is an obvious sign of masochism. Do you find yourself bored when life flows easily? Do you have a story running that says nothing good comes without pain? Balance your life by allowing yourself to experience the good things. It's time to rewrite your story!

Some of the methods identified by Leon Seltzer as useful for transforming people pleaser, passive, yes saying habits include the following:

- Acknowledge and understand the various ways you subordinate your self to others. Try to pinpoint how, when, and with what people you give up your personal power in order to secure the relationship. Become more aware of what your motives are in such instances. Become more sensitive to the cues and triggers that routinely prompt you to take a pacifying, conciliatory position with others.

- Make an intention or commitment to be true to yourself and start making your own needs clearer to people who matter to you. Begin to practice this in your head till such assertiveness begins to feel more real and comfortable to you.

- Put into practice what you've decided to change. Encourage yourself to go outside your emotional comfort zone. Start expressing your thoughts and feelings, wants and needs independent of whether you see the other person as likely to agree with you.

- Do not keep people in your life who lack a sincere interest in your welfare. Become aware that you have the right to minimise, or avoid altogether, people who are unable or unwilling to treat you with the consideration and respect you're entitled to.

- Beware of your tendency to automatically agree with, or defer to, others. Interrupt your automatic response or reflexive reaction and change your compliance programming. Pause before you respond and think less about what the other person wants from you and more about what you want. Remind yourself that your needs are as important as anyone else's.

- Do things for others because you really care about them, not simply because you're afraid they'll abandon you if you don't. Remember that anyone who would desert you if you failed to submit to his or her preferences really is not someone you want in your life, are they?

Chapter 3:
Why do I say Yes when I know I should say No?

I have absolutely no pleasure in the stimulants in which I sometimes so madly indulge. It has not been in the pursuit of pleasure that I have periled life and reputation and reason. It has been the desperate attempt to escape from torturing memories, from a sense of insupportable loneliness and a dread of some strange impending doom.

Edgar Allan Poe

It is really important to understand why you have such a hard time saying NO. Understanding why you do what you do is central to knowing yourself. If you live your life being unable to resist others or indulging in addictive behaviours or being dependent on the approval of others, you will never feel even a degree of independence or happiness. This is because you are basically saying that you cannot live without an object to fill the deep hole inside you. As with almost everything else relating to the human psyche, when a behavioural pattern that was once adaptive as a child is clearly maladaptive as an adult, there will be a strong, deep-seated resistance to changing it. This opposition will hold regardless of how much you consciously desire to change it. Consequently, it's important to anticipate feelings of hesitancy, nervousness, guilt, and ambivalence.

Saying Yes to ways that help us learn new things about ourselves, others and life comes from the place of a good Yes. Yes is the way we build

Chapter 3: Why do I say Yes when I know I should say No?

friendships and connections with others. Saying Yes takes us out of our comfort zone so that we experience change even though it feels a bit uncomfortable. It's worth it because it's also exciting at the same time. But what if you always say Yes to avoid saying NO. What if saying Yes comes from a habit that you can't change. Constantly saying Yes when you want to say NO can leave you vulnerable, stressed and exhausted.

Here is what Chantalle Blickman, author of 'How to Stop Saying Yes When You Want to Say No', says of herself:

> I am a sucker for saying yes. Sometimes I even find myself thinking 'no, no, no, no' and then I blurt out 'yes.' Why is it so difficult to say the word 'no'? It's just a word, right? After feeling trapped for some time by my excessive urge to be agreeable, it got me thinking. I asked myself why it was so important for me to please everyone, to the point that I would feel resentful and stressed because of it. I realized I was afraid of saying no because my biggest fear is rejection. I was afraid that every time I did this, I would disappoint someone, make them angry, hurt their feelings, or appear unkind or rude. Having people think negatively of me is the ultimate rejection. Whether they say what they think of me, out loud or not, does not matter to me. It is the thought that they look down on me. And so I realized exactly why I found it so difficult to say no. I realize this is not just a challenge that I face but also one that many people go through every day. It's a heavy burden to carry because with the urge to say yes also comes a lack of self-confidence and self-value.

You need to stop saying Yes when you really need to be saying NO. But it's important to point out that sometimes NO can appear in the form of a Yes: 'Do you mind if I touch your baby bump?' 'Yes I do mind. Do not touch me'. So you have the right to refuse even when permission is asked.

This is also the good NO and there are many ways to say NO beyond the word NO. When you say a reluctant Yes instead of an honest NO you often feel as though you have let yourself down and, at the same time, you feel resentful towards the person who asked. James Altucher is an American entrepreneur, author, and podcaster; he says that:

> Every time you say yes to something you don't want to do; you will resent people, you will do a bad job, you will have less energy for the things you were doing a good job on, you will make less money, and yet another small percentage of your life will be burned up.

ADDICTION

You know you have an addiction when you are being controlled by something that you absolutely cannot say NO to. Your brakes are not working and you are unable to slow it down. Instead, you accelerate head long into the drama as your life unravels and things spiral into chaos. As a general term, dependence is the state of needing something or someone in order to function or survive. As applied to alcohol and drugs, it means a need

Chapter 3: Why do I say Yes when I know I should say No?

for repeated doses of a substance to feel good or to avoid feeling bad. Regardless of the reason, a person is drawn to alcohol or drugs because it worked for them, at least once in the beginning. You expect certain physical and emotional sensations when you use substances, and this is what keeps the pattern going: the more these expectations of elation, relaxation, happiness, confidence, relief, or any other sensation are fulfilled, the more you want to drink or use drugs. So saying Yes is rewarded until you can't say NO, even if you wanted to.

According to the World Health Organisation (WHO) dependence on drugs or alcohol is defined as the repeated use of a psychoactive substance, to the extent that the user is periodically or chronically intoxicated, shows a compulsion to take the preferred substance, has great difficulty in voluntarily ceasing or modifying the substance use, and exhibits determination to obtain psychoactive substances by almost any means. Typically, tolerance is prominent and a withdrawal syndrome frequently occurs when substance use is interrupted. The life of the addicted person may be dominated by substance use to the virtual exclusion of all other activities and responsibilities. At some point, a transition occurs. The usual sequence does not work in the same way it had in the beginning. Maybe you developed tolerance or started to experience withdrawal symptoms. These symptoms can lead you to drink or use more often so that you feel better. When the symptoms of tolerance or withdrawal begin, this often marks the progression of what started as social or recreational use to problematic use. When you are so preoccupied with drinking or using just to feel okay, other things you used to do with your time fall by the wayside, as you start to spend your time using, recovering from using, and planning to use again. What's more, despite its negative impact on one or more aspects of your life you find yourself blindly continuing to use anyway.

The treatment of addiction is way outside the scope of this book but the reason it is included here is that the inability to say NO is central in addiction, in other words, saying Yes to things you ought to say NO to. The addiction industry goes back and forth over whether addiction is a brain disease or a choice. In either case, it is the addict who must make the decision to take steps to control their addiction. We all make decisions everyday of our lives but in the case of an addiction, the decision to abuse substances is a powerful error of judgment that's made repeatedly. Giving yourself permission to consume to excess repeatedly and thus relinquish responsibility for decision-making is central to addiction.

How is it possible, in these circumstances, to retain the ability to give consent for sex, for instance, let alone anything else? Consent requires voluntary agreement to something that the person clearly understands and expresses an intention to participate in. But a person in an inebriated or drug-affected state cannot surely be giving consent by virtue of not actually saying the word NO. Sexual consent plays an important role in defining what sexual assault is, since sexual activity without consent is rape. Intoxicated consent then is a complex issue in the light of a significant number of sexual assaults that go unreported because of shame and embarrassment, and feeling responsible for the assault. 'I was out of it and I can't really remember much so I guess it was my own fault.'

Denial is a mechanism of defence seen in a person who is faced with a fact that is too uncomfortable for them to accept, so they disavow or reject it, insisting that it's not true despite the overwhelming evidence. The concept of denial is important in addiction where the belief is that substance dependence and its consequences are not a problem. An illustration of this is the claim of being a 'high functioning' user is to deny the changes that have occurred as a result of the addiction. The person is blind to what has been happening to them and desperately wants to hold onto 'not knowing'. Like the Buddhist motto, 'Knowledge at the end of a large piece of wood' as you repeatedly hit yourself over the head before you finally get it, maybe.

Chapter 3: Why do I say Yes when I know I should say No?

Tobacco, alcohol and illicit drug use contribute to increased chronic disease, injury, poisoning and premature death and are among the leading risk factors contributing to disease burden in Australia, according to the 2019 data from the Australian Institute of Health and Welfare. There is no point in prevaricating on this issue of addiction because people are dying in their droves. The World Health Organisation states that alcohol consumption alone causes death and disability mainly in the 20–39 year age group, and approximately 13.5% of total deaths worldwide are attributable to alcohol. These are all very sobering figures. So why can't people say NO to the consumption, in excess, of something that is so bad for them.

It is through the lens of addiction that we see how difficult the good NO is and how complex and deep-seated the reasons are for its failure. Ask the relatives of alcoholics who cajole, beg, and threaten for years and years for them to give up the booze. It is devastating for them to witness the breakdown of their loved one's life. What we are coming to understand here is that NO is anything but simple. So we need to understand the meaning of what is happening to the individual who cannot say NO and the consequences of their dysfunctional choices.

The Internet and Social media

A couple of important factors that contribute to anxiety amongst the young today, according to Psychology Today, are parenting practices that overprotect children and the rise of social media. Advances in technology provide new opportunities for connecting people in modern life, but they also lead to new experiences of negative social comparison and new pathways for social exclusion. How much screen time do you have each day? Do you blink sometimes after being lost inside your device and wonder where you are? We work, we communicate and we play and socialise on our computers, our iPads, our phones, and now on our watches. Our devices, and the digital technology that drives them, take up an extraordinary amount of our daily experience. The internet offers a world of products for consumption in excess. Anything your heart desires can be satisfied. The younger generation have been born into it and take it for granted; two and three year olds have their own iPads. We have instant screen-to-screen communication with Skype, Zoom, and Facetime that saved us during times of COVID quarantine. In the community, on public transport, in restaurants and in cafes most people have their faces in a screen or their mobile phones are right beside them within easy reach. As indicated earlier, you know you have an addiction when you are being controlled by something that you absolutely cannot say NO to. The majority of people do not even turn their phones off at night and have a hard time putting them on silent.

Social media allows users to quickly create and share content with everyone via a wide range of websites and apps. Third party online social media carriers such as Twitter, Facebook, LinkedIn, Instagram, Snapchat and YouTube have become a huge part of our daily existence. We indulge in convenient and instant online social contact with the added thrill of instant feedback. Then there are all the dating apps like: Zoosk, eHarmony, Tinder, Grindr, Hinge, Plentyoffish to name just a few. It's a given

Chapter 3: Why do I say Yes when I know I should say No?

now that the only way to meet someone for fun or for a relationship is online and anonymously. When it comes to internet relationships everyone knows everything about you, well at least what you tell them because fake personas abound online. Social media has the ability to make relationships both easier and more difficult; it can connect us when we are far away, or it can hinder our ability to focus on what truly matters in a relationship. There is growing evidence that social media addiction is an evolving problem, particularly among the young. A correlation exists between prioritising social media image management and a widespread escalation in the experience of anxiety and depression, disrupted sleep and general stress. To what extent does social media affect you? Can you say NO and reduce the amount of time you spend on your devices?

Although social media is largely seen as a positive influence on communication, it is also causing problems that need to be acknowledged:

- Social media sucks up inordinate amounts of time that may previously have been spent more productively
- Personal information invades the public domain resulting in a lack of privacy
- There are concerns over children and teenagers' lack of social skills and neglect of family relationships due to internet use
- Produces social isolation that accentuates feelings of loneliness
- Creates illusory, fake and shallow connections
- It produces jealousy of others and suspicion over partners' online activities, including fears of online cheating
- Concern over personally damaging or detrimental posts, including threats of violence online manifesting themselves offline
- Cyber-bullying, online harassment, and 'trolling'.
- Internet pornography, cybersex and online dating and gambling sites continue to cause problems in relationships

- Unhealthy comparisons between your life and the lives of your friends
- Negative body image comparisons and lack of satisfaction
- Sleep disturbance due to chatting online
- Obsessive checking of social media
- Emotional side effects such as; social media burnout, Facebook depression and FOMO

Rather than saying NO to the seductive pull of capitalist forms of enjoyment, there is a belief in quick fixes in the illusion of an alternate life that will bring happiness. In other words, you're living in la-la land. These issues are the result of First World privilege, that is, any unearned advantages you accrue by virtue of being a member of a First World country in contrast with the difficulties of greater social significance that face people in poor and underdeveloped parts of the world. This may sound a bit harsh and guilt inducing but it is, nonetheless, true.

INTIMACY

Intimacy refers to the experience of closeness and connection in the context of the ability to genuinely share who you are with another person. The fear of intimacy is characterised by the avoidance of and inability to share a close emotional or physical relationship. You may long for closeness, but frequently push others away or even sabotage relationships. Fear of abandonment and fear of being engulfed are at the heart of the fear of intimacy for many people, and these two fears can coexist. Although the fears are very different both cause behaviours that alternately pull the partner in and then push them away again.

People who consistently abuse substances do so to escape the discomfort of life and relationships. Addiction nearly always arises in people with unresolved Adverse Childhood Events (ACEs), psychological disorders, or personality challenges. Issues like childhood trauma, sexual abuse,

Chapter 3: Why do I say Yes when I know I should say No?

depression, anxiety, and attachment disorders cause intense feelings of shame and guilt with a tendency for the person to isolate and avoid social contact. This leads to self-medicating with substances and cross-addictions such as sex, gambling, eating, internet, spending, porn, taking risks and so on. Exacerbating this situation is the fact that most people dealing with underlying intimacy issues begin the process relatively early in life. It is usually during adolescence where the process of emotional growth, required for healthy adult relationships, is stunted. In fact, most substance abusers will tell you that when they enter recovery they feel like they are the emotional age of whatever actual age they were when they started using. They are unable to relate very well to other adults in a healthy way because the addiction started very early and arrested their emotional growth. Others have intimacy problems to begin with, which may well have led to their substance use, which in turn escalates the intimacy issue. Either way, for some, substance abuse and intimacy issues become heavily linked – equal parts of a viciously destructive cycle.

As a substance abuser you often fear and therefore avoid, the basic human need for emotional connection and support. So you exist in emotional exile. Even when you're around other people who love you, you can't reach out. In fact, you will say that you feel most alone when you're in the company of family, friends, and other loved ones. Generally speaking, this occurs because you have learned, usually early in life through neglect, abuse, inconsistency, enmeshment, and distressing experiences, to fear and avoid emotional vulnerability. Thus, you distance yourself from others, turning instead to the temporary but reliable fix you find within addictive behaviours. When you become emotionally needy, stressed, suffer losses, or even feel joyful you turn, automatically and without conscious thought, not to other people but to your addiction. You trust the short-term remedy of emotional distraction and numbing more than other people – even people who clearly love you and care about your wellbeing. Interestingly, when addiction is conceptualised in this way, as an intimacy disorder, we see that the best long-term treatment for addiction is the pursuit of healthy, intimate, ongoing connections. Thus, a fundamental task of healing, once you have broken through denial and established a modicum of sobriety, is developing and maintaining healthy and supportive emotional bonds. It is this approach, not willpower or babysitters or shaming or threatened consequences that is most likely to create lasting sobriety and emotional healing. Saying NO to the crutch of addictive substances and behaviours, and Yes to a life shared with others is the way forward.

SEX, ROMANCE AND CO-DEPENDENCY

> The most painful thing is losing yourself in the process of loving someone too much and forgetting that you are special too.
>
> — Ernest Hemingway

Chapter 3: Why do I say Yes when I know I should say No?

Replace sentence with - Some people seek a sense of personal power and an escape from mental pain in their use of sex as a way to feel better about themselves and in control of their lives. However, sex never satisfies the longing for love and self-respect. The fundamental momentum for sexual addiction is provided by certain core beliefs:

- you do not perceive yourself as a worthwhile person
- others do not care about you and would not meet your needs if they truly knew you.
- you believe that sex is your most important need because it makes isolation bearable.

Patrick Carnes says that, 'If you do not trust people, one thing that is true about sex - and alcohol, drugs, food, gambling, and risk - is that it always does what it promises - for the moment.' This sanctions the belief that in sex addiction, the relationship is generally only with sex and not with a person. In pornography addiction, relationships and daily responsibilities are replaced with pornography. Most pornography addicts are isolated when engaged in their sexual acting-out and will spend hours and days lost in their thoughts over the two-dimensional porn images. They may indulge in online fantasy games to meet their addiction needs or resort to cybersex. Internet porn addicts can also pursue online photography and videos while non-internet porn addicts go to strip clubs or sex shops to satisfy their addiction.

Charlotte Kasl says that female sex and love addiction is manifest differently than in males. Males tend to objectify their partners and prefer sexual behaviour that involves relatively little emotional involvement. Women who are addicted to sex, on the other hand, tend to use sex for power, control, and attention. Unlike men, women seem to be reacting against culturally prescribed norms. What follows is a post entitled 'For all the women who can't say no' - placed on a psych forum on sex addiction (March 2021):

> Ladies, I know you are out there. I started this thread to see if any of you have had the same experience as me. First date-can't say no, guy friend comes over-can't say no, coworker wants to f**k you-can't say no. I shame myself for being like this...some of these guys I don't even want to sleep with but I do anyway. I can't help it. I don't seek it out. But right before the act starts and I have that chance to say no I don't, my mind goes blank in a sense. Sometimes while having sex I'll say no but usually that is ignored and I won't protest anyway. I know a lot of it has to do with my hypersexual state being turned on but not always, a lot of these sexual experiences haven't been the least bit enjoyable. I know a lot of it has to do with low self esteem. How does one overcome something like this? I've tried in the past but nothing I tell myself keeps me from repeating this behaviour. The advice I get from my girlfriends is always the same 'just say no'. Can anyone on here relate to how difficult doing that is??

Sex addiction in women cannot truly be understood without taking into account the interrelationship of addiction and co-dependency. For most women, sexually addictive and sexually co-dependent behaviours are intertwined and reflect basic female conditioning in our society. She is taught that a woman's power is in her sexuality, and yet it is men who often regulate her sexuality. Thus, sex can easily become a basic form of barter; it is the price many women pay for love and the illusion of security.

The reason why the romantic love relationship is so intense and universally sought after is that it appears to offer us liberty from those deep-seated fears and needs that go with the sense of incompleteness we experience

Chapter 3: Why do I say Yes when I know I should say No?

as human beings. When that special relationship comes along it seems to be the answer to all your problems and meets all your needs. At least this is how it appears at first. All the other things that you derived your sense of self from previously become insignificant. You now have a single focal point that replaces them all. The person you are 'in love' with gives meaning to your life, and it is through them that you define your identity. You are whole and no longer a disconnected fragment in an uncaring universe, or so it seems. Charlotte Kasl defines co-dependency as letting one's body be used in order to hold onto a relationship, regardless of whether the woman really wants to have sex.

In general, sex addicts tend to manipulate relationships in order to have sex, whereas sexually co-dependent women manipulate sex in order to keep relationships. Neither group has a clue about true intimacy. It's fair to say that there is a certain amount of co-dependency in all relationships. Among the core characteristics when co-dependency is problematic, is an excessive reliance on the other person for approval and for a sense of identity. Co-dependency involves sacrificing one's personal needs to try to meet the needs of another person. This type of relationship pattern is unbalanced and detrimental. It exists in a relationship where one person enables another person's addiction, poor mental health, immaturity, irresponsibility, or under-achievement. The co-dependent person has an extreme focus on the other person, usually a family member or a partner, and their thoughts and actions revolve solely around them. When co-dependency and addiction occur together, the two behaviours will reinforce one another. If you are co-dependent you will probably have the following indicators:

- Low self-esteem due to deeply held feelings of shame, guilt, inadequacy, and a need for perfection
- A need to make other people happy and an inability to say NO to demands

- Problems creating healthy boundaries and distinguishing responsibility for actions
- A need to control situations, people, and your own feelings
- Poor communication skills
- Obsessively thinking about your own anxieties and fears and those of other people
- Dependency on other people
- Fear of and issues with intimacy
- Uncomfortable and painful feelings such as, depression, resentment, and despair

Co-dependency was first associated with partners of alcoholics and, today, addiction is still one of the most common associations of co-dependency. The Al-Anon Family Groups are a fellowship of relatives and friends of alcoholics who share their experiences in order to deal with their common problems. Alcoholism is thought to be a family illness and Al-Anon holds that changing attitudes can aid recovery. The problematic attitudes that prevail are: excessive care-taking, an inability to differentiate between love, pity and loyalty, fixation on the problems of the alcoholic and unrealistically over-estimating their agency, attempting to control the other person's drinking behaviour and, when this fails, blaming themselves for the other person's behaviour.

We are all unique individuals who experience life differently. We are not united together as one being and we never will be; we are all separate people. Scary as it sounds you are fundamentally alone on this earth. As Orson Welles said: 'We are born alone, we live alone and we die alone'. Get used to it. Family and relationships help but they can be hard work because we have to negotiate and communicate and listen and accommodate and explain and give and take, etc. Respecting differences helps us get along with those we love, care about or at least like.

Chapter 3: Why do I say Yes when I know I should say No?

We develop the capacity to be with people through discernment and by using self-discipline; it's like another muscle that needs to be built up with practice over time. We don't always get it right but in a secure trusting relationship it's okay to keep trying.

CONSENT AND THE MEANING OF NO

The song 'I Can't Say No' is from the Rodgers and Hammerstein 1943 musical called *Oklahoma*. It's about a girl who can't say NO to the temptation of men, even though she knows she should refuse and her inability to say NO gets her into trouble. It goes like this:

> It ain't so much a question of not knowing what to do;
>
> I've knowed what's right and wrong since I've been ten!
>
> I've heard a lot of stories, and I reckon they are true,
>
> About how girls are put upon by men.
>
> I know I mustn't fall into the pit,
>
> But when I'm with a feller.....I forget!
>
> I'm just a girl who can't say no,
>
> I'm in a terrible fix
>
> I always say, 'Come on, let's go'
>
> Just when I ought to say nix!
>
> When a person tries to kiss a girl,
>
> I know she ought to give his face a smack.
>
> But as soon as someone kisses me,
>
> I somehow, sort of, want to kiss him back!
>
> I'm just a fool when lights are low

> I can't be prissy and quaint
> I ain't the type that can faint
> How can I be what I ain't?
> I can't say no!

Your capacity to give or withhold consent is intrinsically linked to your sense of agency. Before being sexual with someone, you need to know if they want to be sexual with you too. It's important to be honest about what you want and don't want. Consenting and asking for consent are all about setting your personal boundaries and respecting those of your partner. Both people must agree to sex every single time for it to be consensual. Without consent, any sexual activity is sexual assault or rape. This is the type of sexual assault at the highest risk of being normalised or dismissed as 'just a part of life'. It is dangerous when women are unable to identify that what they're experiencing is wrong, much less illegal. The line between consensual compliance and non-consensual coercion gets fuzzy when women agree to things they wouldn't have if they had felt more empowered to decline. Bordering on coercion is a category of experience that researchers call compliance: having sex that you don't particularly want but are not being directly pressured to accept. Having some clarity around what kind of touch interests you and feels good helps people to be more explicit about the acts that feel wrong.

JANE

Jane is a young woman in her mid 20's. Life feels hard for her right now. The skills she learned from previous therapies no longer work. For the last year she has progressively felt that life is not worth living. She is employed and has a great husband; they are planning to start a family, but Jane is not up for that any more. She has been avoiding friends and has no interests, no passion and no joy. Her husband's

Chapter 3: Why do I say Yes when I know I should say No?

touch triggers her and she can't stand it. Jane keeps stuff bottled up and always has. She finds it awkward talking to friends about personal things. For her, people are hard work and she withdraws from them but at the same time wants to please them. She's not able to say No to anything anyone asks of her. Her moods are all over the place now as she struggles to make sense of herself.

Janes parents married young because they were pregnant and divorced when she was three. She is an only child but both parents went on to have more children after they re-partnered. Jane lived between both parents in a shared custody arrangement. She did not fit in anywhere with either family and did not feel affirmed by anyone close to her. At primary school she described herself as socially unable and afraid of other kids. 'They didn't like me so I learned to be a people pleaser. I need to be liked. I studied them so I could understand what they wanted and I became that person. I pretended to be someone they would like.'

The first time Jane was sexually coerced was when sleeping over at a school friend's house at the age of 13. The friend had a 15-year-old brother and they all slept in the same room. This boy put her hand on his penis. She felt embarrassed and didn't know what to do so she did nothing. Another time he got into her bed and touched her sexually. She couldn't tell him to stop and felt ashamed. She thought that not saying No meant that she deserved what happened. After all her efforts to be liked she became hypersensitive and imagined that the whole family rejected her. Over the ensuing years Jane found that she couldn't say No to the advances of men she encouraged, and it didn't occur to her to ask if sex was what she wanted or not. She was always either drunk or wasted on drugs. The day after each encounter she felt ashamed and degraded, hating herself for allowing this to happen, again. She thought her troubles might have been over when she met and then married her husband but, of course, she brought them with her.

The Good No

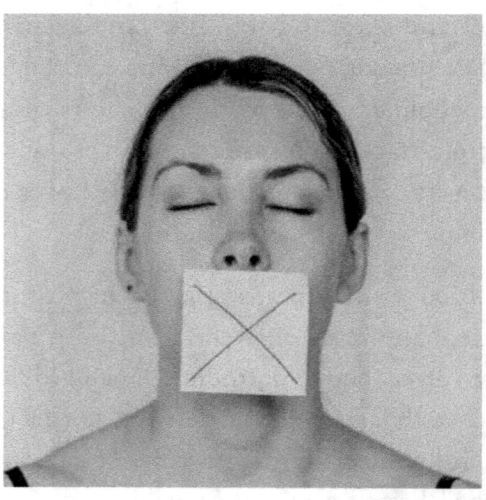

The #MeToo movement is a social movement aimed at empowering sexually assaulted individuals through strength in numbers by visibly demonstrating how many have survived sexual assault and harassment. Following the exposure of widespread sexual abuse allegations against Harvey Weinstein in 2017 the movement went viral as a hashtag on social media. The #MeToo movement circulated broadly especially on Twitter as a way for people, particularly women, to publicly identify themselves as having experienced sexual harassment, coercion or assault. This movement brought to light the fact that the majority of sexual assaults are not the result of misunderstandings or misinterpreting consent but with cultural norms that encourage men to go ahead in its absence. There is a difference between not understanding someone's NO, and understanding it but feeling entitled to make it a YES anyway. The task of sexual assault prevention is largely being left to women; it remains the responsibility of potential victims to defend themselves rather than of perpetrators to control and take responsibility for their own behaviour.

#MeToo, although freeing women and men to report harassment and abuse, has resulted in significant confusion and disorientation for people entering romantic or sexual relationships. Consent may ultimately be about people giving themselves the right to consent; to think in the moment about whether a sexual encounter is something they want, and to give themselves permission to call it off if they find it is not. Sexual harassment, unlike rape, is a project of leisurely objectification that depends, for its erotic charge, on the perversion of consent. Unlike rape where consent is vanquished, or erotic mutuality where it is endorsed, the pleasure of sexual harassment is that consent is coerced, that is, it is consent under duress. Under these conditions, which slowly dismantle the identity of the victim, the issue becomes one of reality testing. 'Just say no' is not an option when the question at hand is 'What just happened?' In Australia sexual harassment is unlawful under the Sex Discrimination Act and some types of sexual harassment may be considered a criminal offence. This is particularly pertinent to the Sex Discrimination Commissioner review of Parliamentary workplaces mentioned in the introduction.

THE BEAUTY INDUSTRY

Beauty is a currency system like the gold standard. Like any economy, it is determined by politics, and in the modern age in the West it is the last, best belief system that keeps male dominance intact.

The Beauty Myth by Naomi Wolf (1991)

Realistically speaking, humans have access to more beauty enhancing products and services than ever before in history. The world of beauty attracts many and for some it is an addiction. We are force-fed on the details of how superstars, celebrities and the beautiful people live; where they go on holiday, how they dress, what makeup they use, their weight loss tips and how much so and so spent on cosmetic surgery to win her man back, it never stops. These people are held up as icons for our consumption and it's fuelled by an ever more intrusive paparazzi because, after all, we read the stories and gaze at the photos. The media has great power in the way it impacts and distorts our perception of beauty in 21st century society. We scrutinise the female form everywhere; models on magazine covers and in advertising, social media influencers who show off in order to sell stuff online, the way a woman's body is portrayed in movies and all over our screens on television, Facebook and especially Instagram. Of course men's bodies are exposed too but not nearly as much or as often as women's. For every single perceived flaw that a woman has there is a solution sold to correct that exaggerated imperfection. The images used to promote health and beauty are airbrushed and digitally enhanced, therefore the notion of health and beauty that we ascribe to is in fact impossible and unachievable. We are not talking about real human beings here but inanimate ageless Ken and Barbie dolls. In this way the beauty trade and media have created a homogenised version of beauty. The industries interpretation of what constitutes beauty has become a dominant paradigm for vulnerable individuals who judge themselves and those around them as seriously lacking.

Beauty enhancement solutions are being taken up by younger and younger men and women to prevent them ever developing the horrors of crows-feet on their porcelain smooth faces. A booming anti-aging culture is dependent on us feeling uncomfortable with the aging process, and much less able to embrace it. The success and profitability of the companies that benefit from this culture are directly linked to our insecurities and desire to turn back a clock that will tick away regardless. This is a culture that asks us to conflate health and wellness with youth and beauty selling us the idea that aging and wellness do not coexist. Advances in medical and cosmetic technologies have brought on waves of new ideas around beauty where commercial interests, both in the media and the health industry,

Chapter 3: Why do I say Yes when I know I should say No?

spurred by fashion, advertising and celebrity promotion, have tended to popularise body modifications and enhancements.

Propaganda has become entangled with health advice to make beauty sound very appealing when, in fact, it's a subterfuge that promotes the belief that if you look good then you must be good even if you don't necessarily feel good. We are told that watching our diet will keep us slim and that exercise keeps our hearts fit; we take supplements and vitamins to promote health and sport a nice spray tan to give the look that we have just returned from a trip to Queensland. The thigh gap is an invented body shape that is responsible for a spate of eating disorders around the world. We need surgery to remove unwanted fat and flab or to tighten folds of flesh that have slackened indicating the passage of time. Age has become the enemy and aging women are pitied for letting themselves go. What you cannot be is hairy, fat and ageing. There was a time in the 1960's when hairy armpits and braless breasts were considered quite sexy. Removing body hair was very much a fashion choice, but increasingly, people see body hair removal as a hygiene practice, and body hair as abnormal and unnatural.

A Brazilian butt-lift will create that Kardashian profile with breast implants, body sculpting and complete hairlessness to balance the look. For the mouth there is the 'trout pout' where fat is taken from your bum and injected into your lips giving the impression of a fish; your teeth get straightened and whitened so you can flash a great smile; your nose is reshaped to perky perfection; and your eyes resurfaced, remodelled and augmented with eyebrow lamination and an eyelash lift with the final addition of fake eyelashes that frankly come straight out of Rocky Horror Picture Show. Your body can be marked and engraved with tattoos and piercings to emphasise your identity.

The choices around cosmetic make up, surgery and enhancements are vast. Available to you is a vast array of products and procedures specifically designed for all your skincare needs. Firstly, every wrinkle must be smoothed out with the injection of a neurotoxin protein called Botox until, like a statue, nothing moves on the face, not a muscle twitches to indicate an emotion, which can be quite disconcerting to witness. There are various anti-wrinkle facials and peels, dermal filler injections for your creases, and platelet rich plasma injections for something else, who knows. There is microdermabrasion and laser skin resurfacing to burn off pigmentation and those age-betraying marks and spots to ensure the surface of your face is polished, shiny and new. It's hard to find a bit of the body that isn't under scrutiny as an area of concern and in need of being rectified. Who is all this beautification for? Who is looking, judging and evaluating you? Can you say NO to that?

We have hardly even begun to discuss the domains into which beauty commerce has infiltrated. As a woman if you are displeased with your genital area you can have all kinds of things done to improve the situation, including your sexual enjoyment. This is due to the increasing pull of pornography where vaginal comparisons have created a whole new market for consumers. You can have your vagina tightened so you're like a virgin again and while you're there you can have both it and your anus whitened, of course you will have your pubic hair deforested with wax or laser and then 'vajazzled' with Swarovski crystals. If you'd like to go a step further, you can venture into genital surgery and opt for a 'Barbie'. This involves the amputation of the labia minora resulting in a smooth, flawless 'clamshell' appearance, just like a Barbie doll. Female genital cosmetic surgery refers to a group of non-medically indicated cosmetic surgical procedures that change the structure and appearance of the healthy external genitalia of women. More specifically Simonis et al (2016) tell us that this form of surgery encompasses labiaplasty (trimming of the labia minora and less commonly labia majora), hymenoplasty (hymen repair), vaginoplasty (vaginal reconstruction), mons pubis liposuction, vaginal rejuvenation, G-spot augmentation and O-shot. The Orgasm-shot is a series of injections to the clitoris, labia majora, labia minora, and anterior wall of the vaginal mucosa to improve orgasm, vaginal lubrication, urinary stress incontinence, and libido enhancement. G-spot enhancements are injections to the G-spots in the vagina to create intense and deeper orgasms.

Masses of women are flocking to this new form of voluntary genital mutilation/alteration for many reasons; it is the fastest-growing cosmetic operation in the world following liposuction (fat removal), breast augmentation (boob implants) and rhinoplasty (nose jobs). The global cosmetic surgery market is expected to reach $43.9 billion by 2025. Cosmetic surgery is popular worldwide, and Australia ranks in the top ten countries spending the most money. According to statistics from the Victorian Cosmetic Institute, Australia spent one billion dollars on cosmetic surgery in 2017. The Zoom Boom during COVID lockdowns is driving interest in cosmetic procedures that correct the facial expressions lines and wrinkles we notice on video calls. There's currently a surge in demand for 'neck rejuvenation' and 'jawline contouring', as people spend more time looking down the lens of their computer camera.

Plastic surgery addiction is a behavioural obsession characterised by the compulsion to continuously alter one's appearance with cosmetic surgery. In addition to the physical and mental health concerns associated with plastic surgery addiction, it has also been connected to opioid abuse. This addiction most often stems from underlying insecurities that are fed by cultural and societal messages encouraging the individual to believe that they should be someone other than who they are. We humans have a powerful drive for social acceptance and it's very difficult to resist a perception about beauty that's reinforced relentlessly in the media. Many people go to extreme measures to obtain perfect breasts, chin, lips and face but there is no such thing as a perfect body or a perfect face. Body dysmorphia is a mental illness characterised by an intense focus on appearance and body image where the person sees himself or herself as ugly, malformed, misshapen, or hideous. People with body dysmorphia repeatedly check themselves in the mirror and may seek numerous cosmetic procedures to try to correct the apparent flaw. They may feel temporary satisfaction or a reduction in distress afterwards, but soon the anxiety returns, and they resume searching for other ways to correct their apparent deficiencies. We can say that these people are not only obsessed but also possessed by the continual pursuit of supposed perfection.

Quora is a social question-and-answer website based in California. A question, 'Why is there an obsession with anti-aging and being young?' was posted on Quora and a student replied with the following response:

> I'm obsessed with anti aging because I look young and pretty, and my whole life it's how I got what I wanted. I wanted love and a nice guy to take me places and have fun with and enjoy life. The reason my boyfriend picked me is because of how I look. He loves showing me off. The best feeling in the world is when he caresses my face and stares at me in admiration. I know he won't dare hurt me because I can see he is crazy about me and my looks make him giggly and happy rather than mean and harsh. I can't lose that. I'm not afraid of death whatsoever actually I've attempted suicide twice and the third time I will try with a bullet to my head. That's for when I start looking old though because I won't watch my beauty fade and live through the pain of becoming invisible and then die anyway. That makes no sense. So instead of being a procrastinator, I'll just end my life fast. Until then, I'm on mega doses of anti-aging vitamins and a whole regiment of expensive creams as well as drinking my weight in water daily.

Chapter 3: Why do I say Yes when I know I should say No?

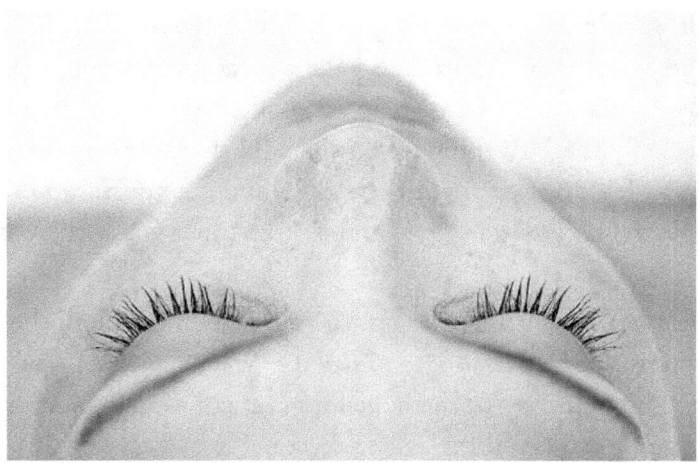

When faced with the loss of youth we get terrified that the best years are behind us. What if you could see your life as something that continued to be full of possibilities, opportunities, and adventure? This fear prevents you from embracing the changes and mystery the journey ahead may present. Here are a few suggestions to help with this fear:

- Practice gratitude by appreciating what you have rather than what you don't have. What have you accomplished in your years on this earth? What are you grateful for thus far in life? You will most likely find that your greatest accomplishments and sources of gratitude have come with age.
- Be health conscious by eating well, have a good night's sleep and exercise appropriately but don't get obsessed with it.
- Build your relationships with family and friends and neighbours and colleagues and others. Don't be afraid to connect.
- Honour your loved ones who have died before you by living life to the fullest and building a legacy. Let go of unrealistic expectations and refrain from comparing yourself to others. It's a waste of time and makes you feel bad about yourself.

- Do not be afraid to take a long hard look at yourself, including your face and your body. Appreciate your appearance as you age, including those smile lines that give you character, the boobs that sag a bit and the belly that's swelling with time, and that scar on your left knee where you fell over when you were eight and cut yourself on a piece of glass. Now look into your eyes and see the inner you – there is a story there for you to tell.
- Look forward as you age, perhaps to your retirement or all the exciting travel plans that lie ahead after COVID. Maybe it's the hope of seeing your children grow up or the hope for grandchildren in older age or the novel that's in you, waiting to be written.
- Exercise your intellect by learning to do something new like play bridge and speak a language or by reading more broadly, doing the Sudoku or cryptic crosswords. Stretch your mind.
- Nurture your creativity by taking up craft or painting or pottery, for example. Use your imagination.
- Take time out to be still or do meditation, or grow a vegetable patch, or go bushwalking, and on it goes.
- Learn to live life fully and to your heart's desire. Understand that there's more to life than your suffering right now. What else do you want to do in your life? Stop making excuses and start now. Make an impact on the world. Life's too short for rules - go and break a few.
- If you still find yourself obsessed with the youth and beauty myth it's time to go and talk to someone sensible.

▶▶▶
Chapter 4:
Healthy Mind and The Good No

There is no witness so terrible and no accuser so powerful as conscience, which dwells within us
Sophocles (497-406 BC)

Why is it that some of us find it so hard to defend ourselves, either in the sense of answering someone back who has bad intentions towards us, or of not falling apart inside in the face of criticism or an attack? Why is it that, when being bullied at work, some people are able to mount a polite but firm comeback, while others melt into shame and despair? Why is it that if you are chastised unfairly by a lover, you might be able to point out that it was unjust and tell your side of the story in a way that's steady and solid, while others might descend into defensiveness and paranoia? To be able to take care of or defend yourself against an external threat, you have to be on your own side because if your entire personality is geared towards interpreting yourself as bad, wrong, a mistake, shameful or a piece of shit you have no stable ground to fight back from. If the fundamental truth about yourself is negative, you will be mentally vulnerable in the face of opposition. This can lead to a crisis where you need to take on board the fact that the real enemy is not on the outside, but on the inside.

Battles of the mind are common for us all, albeit they may differ in form and intensity from person to person. These are struggles that cause a degree of suffering without manifesting in external symptoms that are either severe enough or specific enough to meet mental illness diagnostic criteria. For example, some of you may avoid interpersonal conflict due to an unconscious fear that you will lose the love or support of others. For some, this may be a minor issue that causes stress when you feel driven to defend an idea or to stand up for yourself. For others, it may be more incapacitating, causing them to agree to things they feel unhappy about and then resent the situation they find themselves in. This resentment might, in turn, lead to feelings of unhappiness or it might simply be the source of niggling distress. Further along the continuum, the deeply entrenched fear that conflict will bring disastrous consequences, such as complete abandonment by a loved one, will result in relationship problems and the development of stress related symptoms. It's all the same basic issue that's experienced at varying levels of intensity, causing differing levels of distress and varying degrees of dysfunction.

A mental health diagnosis becomes more possible at the further end of the continuum, but the diagnosis itself is unlikely to reflect the complexity of the underlying problem or to amend the distress it causes, even though talking about and naming the problem may have been helpful and comforting. Mental health is a key component of overall health and wellbeing. According to the Australian Institute of Health and Welfare (AIHW), mental health includes your emotional, psychological, and social wellbeing that affects how you think, feel, and act. Your mental health also helps determine how you handle stress, relate to others, and make choices. Hence, a mental illness can be defined as an umbrella term that covers a range of clinically diagnosable disorders that significantly interferes with a person's cognitive, emotional or social abilities. The true prevalence of mental illness globally remains relatively unknown because mental health is typically under-reported, misunderstood and under-diagnosed. In 2017 the AIHW informs us that around 1:7, that's one billion people globally, had one or more mental or substance use disorders, the largest numbers with an anxiety disorder.

Chapter 4: Healthy Mind and The Good No

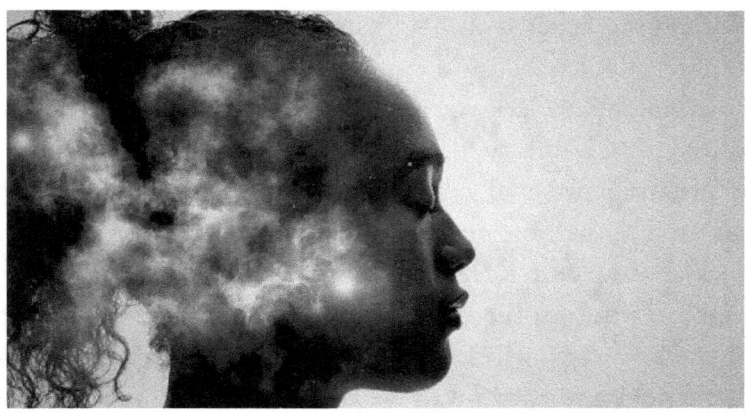

This book is not directed towards diagnosing or treating mental illness. It is about the madness of everyday life that we all experience. The ordinary everyday madness, to which we are all subject in varying degrees, is usually formed in the crucible of our earliest relationship experiences. These common internal struggles that are generally centred on intimacy, trust and identity underpin why the good NO can be so difficult to invoke for some. We are all entitled to the freedom that comes from knowing and understanding our inner world and hence being able to live more meaningful authentic lives and experience more rewarding relationships. So how and why do these internal struggles manifest themselves so often?

Personal ethics and values

Becoming aware of your actions and how you affect others is revealed in how your ethics and values are explored and integrated into every aspect of your life. Ethics are the set of moral rules that govern your behaviour as a person who is a member of a social group. Ethics determine what is right or wrong in your eyes, and in this way are linked to your conscience. Your conscience is the assessment you make of your behaviour that's based on your conformity to what is perceived by you as proper moral conduct. Your values determine what is important to you; they are the beliefs you hold as an enduring preference that acts as a standard of behaviour. Values set your priorities in life and are the reason behind the choices you make. These values might be honesty, respect, integrity, humility, discipline, responsibility, and compassion, for example. Your personal values are a central part of who you are and who you want to be. They significantly affect your emotional state of mind because values are forces that cause you to behave in certain ways. So, if you are true to your values and you make your choices accordingly, then the way you live will express your core values. This means that your actions and your words are congruent with how you represent yourself.

Identifying and understanding your values is a challenging and important exercise. By becoming more aware of these important factors in your life, you can use them as a guide to make the best choice in any given situation. Some of life's decisions are really about determining what you value most. When many options seem reasonable, it's helpful and comforting to rely on your values and use them as a strong guiding force that points you in the right direction. When you honour your core values consistently you experience fulfilment, and when you don't you will feel out of sync and more likely to escape into old habits, such as regressing into childish or self-destructive behaviours. An example might be a man who grew up in a catholic family where marriage is seen as a sacred vow that he believes in, but he finds himself out on a date knowing that he is betraying his wife and children who are at home thinking that he is working late.

Values are usually fairly stable, yet they don't have strict limits or boundaries. As you move through life your values usually change. An illustration of this is when you start a career and experience success your values may be measured by money and status. However, with changing circumstances such as having a family, work-life balance may cause your values to change and mature. As your definition of success changes, so do your personal values. This is why keeping in touch with your values is a lifelong exercise that informs what you say Yes to and what you say No to. You should continuously revisit your values, especially if you start to feel unbalanced and can't figure out why. As human beings we are quite complex creatures with behaviours that are hard to make sense of, psychoanalytic theory can offer some insights as to why this is.

The Superego

According to Sigmund Freud's psychoanalytic theory of personality, the superego is the component of personality that comprises internalised ideals that we acquire from authority figures, like our parents, teachers and society. The superego has a long evolution in psychoanalytic thinking so, in short, without exploring the depths of Freud's theories, the superego is the latest of Freud's developments of the human personality that features the agencies of the id, the ego and the superego. Our superego evolves during the first three to five years of life in concert with the dissolution of the Oedipus Complex. This occurs as a result of a child's identification with his or her parents and the process of internalising their moral standards. The developing superego absorbs the traditions of the family and society at large; it serves to control aggressive and socially unacceptable impulses, ideally.

In psychoanalysis, conscience is the part of your superego that judges you r actions and thoughts, and then sends that information to the ego for consideration. In 1926 Sigmund Freud wrote about the excessive role the superego can take in neurotic disorders as follows, 'the superego becomes exceptionally severe and unkind, and the ego, in obedience to the superego, produces strong reaction formations in the shape of conscientiousness, piety and cleanliness' (p. 115). The superego criticises, prohibits, and inhibits a person's conscience but it also promotes their positive aspirations and ideals that represent their idealised self-image or ego ideal. The ego ideal is often thought of as the image we have of our ideal selves - the people we want to become. It is this image of the ideal individual, often modelled after people that we know, that we hold up as the standard of who we are striving to be. You can already see just how many things could go wrong at this stage of development to upset the emergence of a healthy superego.

Any violation of the superego's ethical standards will result in feelings of guilt or anxiety and a need to atone for one's actions. It carries out its work of censorship either consciously or unconsciously. The superego has a relationship with the symbolic law that regulates our behaviour and yet, paradoxically, we crumble when its blind authoritarian nature emerges. So the superego has several parts; on one hand it can be a law abiding and principled conscience, and on the other hand it can have excessive and oppressive, senseless and destructive character. When our conscience is out of balance, a domineering superego interferes with how we adhere to our values because our superego acts as an internal judge that criticises and condemns our every move. It leaves you second guessing yourself and has you at the mercy of something that demands more from you than you can give, leaving you diminished if you fail to live up to its standards. The superego focuses its unused aggressivity and turns it on the ego of the individual i.e., your self. For some people punitive archetypes are manifest in the guise of the internalised voice of the parents. These injunctions of the superego haunt the minds of the average person with what they should and shouldn't do, think or say. Thus self-criticism, self-contempt and self-denigration can become second nature and frequently go unquestioned.

As a member of the human herd you assess certain signs as evidence of a person's success such as; the type of car they drive, what kind of job they have, what school they went to, the value of the house they

Chapter 4: Healthy Mind and The Good No

live in, what their partner looks like and on it goes. How you compare yourself, whether favourably or not, is dependent on societal norms. We live in a society that judges its participants and closely measures success and failure. An ordinary life is assessed as being below par because you are expected to live an extraordinary life. These expectations can make people feel ashamed and inadequate. Worth or lack of worth rests on a scale of judgment that feeds on stereotypes and prejudice that can simply be a fickle trend that's popular one day and not the next. It can do your head in! Be aware that societal norms are notoriously unstable and what happens when societal norms join forces with your critical superego?

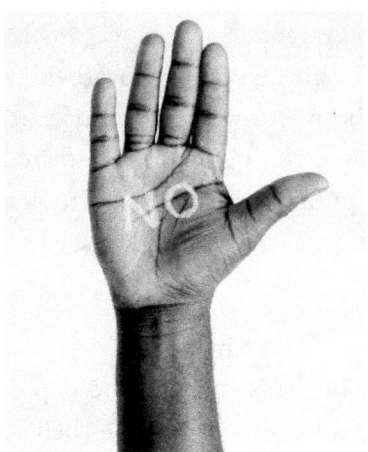

SELF-CRITICISM

Self-critical perfectionism is another manifestation of the super ego that's likely to lead to painful emotional and behavioural states, such as misery, avoidance, angst, and self-condemnation. You will do anything to avoid being quiet or alone and exposed to the content of your own mind. How do you overcome a cruel inner voice that's punitive, panic ridden, and defeatist? You can hear your inner voice mocking or degrading you. Internal voices that tell you that you're not good enough usually come from what has been directed towards you as a child. This can also happen at times when you were vulnerable and believed that the people you trusted turned against you, even if it was unintentional.

Simon is a 60 year old man; he's a lawyer who was a serious alcoholic in his youth but he managed to kick the habit and has been sober for 20 years. In that time he remarried, became religious and successfully reengaged with his three grown up children. However, his unforgiving conscience always hounded him with criticism and he constantly thought that he was a failure. He responded to this by being tireless in his work and on top of that he volunteered at a youth shelter as a way of compensating. He took on more and more, and when anybody asked anything of him he would comply straight away. He was unable to say NO to others and was at the mercy of his demanding overbearing superego. He didn't realise how unhappy he was until he started checking out bottle shops and before long he was drinking again. He feared his wife finding out and couldn't stand the guilt so he impulsively took an overdose and ended up in hospital. His wife was alarmed because she had seen no sign that anything was wrong.

Psychologically speaking, excessive self-criticism is shown to be associated with higher levels of stress, anxiety and depression. And how could it not be? Most people, like Simon, assume their thinking is a mirror of reality so if you are frequently self-critical, you are likely to believe the things you say to yourself. You can get away with a small amount of self-criticism, if you use it as a reality check. However, self-criticism has a way of becoming a habit where, over time the voice gets louder and more believable. Self-criticism induces guilt, telling you how inadequate or flawed you are and this induces shame. With guilt you feel that you have done something wrong, but with shame you feel you are wrong as a person. Shame paralyses you into inaction where you can get really stuck. On the surface, you seem to function well, but shame robs you of feeling good about your achievements. Being highly self-critical takes away the space to self-reflect and to learn. It can take you to really dark places as it did with Simon.

The key to valuing yourself or self-esteem is the way you think and feel about yourself. Check in on yourself with the good NO in mind. How many times in a day do you say: I should, I could, I must, I should have, If only I, I will never be as good as, I should have known better, I could have been more proactive, I should have done more? Do you have an inner voice that chastises you with: you are inadequate, you're an idiot, you can't do anything right, you are not good enough, you are useless, you are a fraud, you are unlovable, you are a loser, you're a failure? Or maybe that inner voice is very subtle attacking strategically without warning, like a terrorist. In any event, self-criticism may be affecting you negatively if you know that you:

1. Have a hard time opening up to people.
2. Are eager to please or need to be a giver.
3. Take everything personally.
4. Are a big procrastinator.
5. Know your critical inner voice is hurting you.
6. Get overly defensive when criticised.
7. Are self-effacing and embarrassed by compliments.
8. Rarely take time out and ignore your health.
9. Are highly critical of others.
10. Don't let others know what you want and need.
11. Feel hopeless, unimportant or alone.
12. Do not expect your needs to be met.
13. Feel too obligated or excessively guilty.
14. Believe that you are a fake or a fraud.

How to do it differently:

- Develop self-awareness and be awake to your critical inner voice. Challenge it regularly in a balanced way. Ask a friend to help with this.
- Meditate by setting aside at least 5-10 minutes 3 times a day to sit quietly by yourself. Tune into your inner self and notice what it is saying. Just be aware and do not judge it or tell it to go away. Simply notice its presence and let it go. Then slowly try to locate the voice (that is part of you) that is respectful, considerate and does not attack you as a person. This can help you focus on your behaviour, not you as a person, and can provide specific insights, shedding light on both your strengths and weaknesses. If the voice is vague, harsh, unbalanced, and attacking acknowledge its origins - gently say NO and allow it to pass by.
- Develop compassion - for yourself and others. You cannot re-write the past but you can certainly begin to allow yourself something of what you may not have received as a child.
- Stay connected with others who you trust. As humans, we are hard-wired to form close bonds. Choose to spend time with people who are authentic and help you feel good about yourself (and you them).
- Seek the help of a good therapist who is professionally trained and accredited. The therapeutic relationship will offer you an opportunity to discover yourself and the meaning of your issues.

Chapter 4: Healthy Mind and The Good No

SELF-PITY

Nobody loves me, everybody hates me Think I'll go and eat worms Long, thin, skinny ones; short, fat, juicy ones See them wiggle and squirm

John Schumann

Feeling sorry for yourself is normal and, in some instances, can serve as a natural stepping-stone to developing acceptance of the difficulties or failures you may have experienced. However, many people make a habit of or indulge in self-pity either as a way to avoid taking personal responsibility, to avoid taking action or simply to gain attention from other people in the form of sympathy. You gather supporters but in the process create a self-fulfilling prophecy by ultimately exhausting and then alienating the previously supportive people. You tend to have a melodramatic streak, are self-absorbed and take yourself far too seriously. This way of operating is very habit forming because it gives you the momentary pleasure of being supported and cared for. But it is maladaptive to make emotional bonds and connections this way as it reinforces an unhealthy cycle of negative thoughts, uncomfortable feelings, and inactivity. Problems are overestimated and the ability to cope is underestimated. It's no wonder then that self-pitying people imagine the worst-case scenarios - like their life will be ruined forever.

The question is how can you stop feeling sorry for yourself and take necessary action? Two exercises that can help build self-reliance are:

1. Act contrary to your self-pity. If you find yourself heading down the road of self-pity, pull back - say NO - and start work on figuring out solutions to your real-life problems. Rather than focusing on the unfairness of your circumstances, remember that everyone has problems of their own and yours is no more important

than theirs. So in order to change the outcome you need to get up off the couch and get moving. Physical activity is so important for your emotional and mental health. Be creative. Regardless of what you do, moving your body can shift and improve your mindset. For instance, you might think about doing something kind for someone else for a change. Help a friend or do volunteer work. Kind acts remind you how much you have to give to others. This can keep you from focusing on what you think other people should be doing for you.

2. Exchange self-pity for gratitude. Instead of thinking 'It's not fair, I deserve better' exchange it for 'I'm thankful for what I do have'. Gratitude is an easiest way to conquer feelings of self-pity because it offers a variety of benefits, including better sleep, improved health, better resilience to stress, and mental strength. Every time you are tempted to complain about how bad your situation is, take positive action and think about three things you're grateful for.

Overachievers

Overachieving is not the same thing as striving to be your best. Overachievers don't want to be seen to be shirking their fair share so they overcompensate by being competitive and outdoing others, so they can take the credit. They want acknowledgement for their contributions and constantly take on extra workloads; stay back after work and panic about the workload they have taken on, including the unrealistic deadlines. Being in control of the situation is central to their modus operandi. Overachievers have to do everything themselves. If you want a job done you have to do it yourself.

People who strive for perfection out of feelings of inadequacy or failure may find it helpful to speak with a therapist to help them manage excessive self-criticism and to take on a more balanced perspective on what's possible and what's impossible. Factors that can contribute to perfectionism and overachieving are the frequent fear of disapproval from others or feelings of insecurity and inadequacy. Added to this are issues like anxiety or obsessionality. You know that you are a part of this group when you:

- Are unable to perform a task unless you know you can do it perfectly.
- Do not focus on the process of learning or completing a task to the best of your ability but view the end product as the most important part of any undertaking.
- Do not see a task as finished until the result is perfect according to your standards.
- Procrastinate by putting off a task until you know you can do it perfectly.
- Take an excessive amount of time to complete a task that does not typically take others that long to complete.
- Compare yourself unfavourably and unrealistically to others.
- Have trouble being happy for others who are successful.
- Even when you get the best results, you may still be dissatisfied.

Parents who model perfectionistic behaviour or express disapproval when their children's efforts are not 100% flawless are a serious problem for their children. An insecure early attachment may result in a person having difficulty self-soothing as an adult or have trouble accepting a good outcome as good if it's not perfect. People with a history of high achievement sometimes feel overwhelming pressure to live up to their previous achievements. If you feel you may have traits of perfectionism that cause you daily distress, know that perfectionistic behaviour and overachieving habits can be changed. It is possible to learn healthier attitudes about your goals and standards with help.

FAKING IT

In a typical day most of us put on a performance pretending that everything is all right. You wake up feeling as though you could do with an extra couple of hours in bed but you drag yourself through the shower and get on with the day. You present yourself positively to others showing them that you are leading a happy fulfilling life, and some of us are, but some of us definitely are not. For a lot of us, our waking lives involve walking on eggshells around others, biting our tongue or smiling when we feel irritated or angry. But when you find yourself presenting a polished shell of who you are rather than your authentic you, what you are really doing is offering the world a façade or a fake version of yourself. Are you the kind of person that when something goes wrong you are more likely to blame yourself than anyone else? Things that went wrong are your fault, you should have known better, or you are responsible for the way the other person acted. Do you compare yourself to others in a reproachful negative way? You have the critical, scolding authoritarian voice of your superego coming at you all the time, looking over your shoulder, wagging its finger at you, judging your every move. Under such a steady scrutiny you try even harder not to screw up, to be even nicer but whatever you do is never good enough. It's always your fault, you are in the wrong again and it's you making all the mistakes. This kind of inner assault is a miserable way to live and it builds resentment.

Inevitably, the tyranny of niceness has expectations and, ultimately resentment has consequences. Those closest to you may experience you as subtly controlling as your thin guise starts to crack and you guilt trip them so that you get your own way. Or you ostensibly go along with something and then act in passive-aggressive mode because your unhappiness is starting to leak out and you target others. Over time your internal system starts to breakdown, a bit at a time. You may become indecisive, there may be signs of burnout and fatigue or you get sick or sink into misery.

Chapter 4: Healthy Mind and The Good No

Rather than clearly stating what you want at the start, you anticipate or assume what the other person would like, you downplay your own needs but still expecting them to know, and over time you find yourself living a sterile life. Close relationships become stale, lack depth and are inauthentic. Your life becomes ordinary, you have lingering regrets, you are never truly known by anyone, and are left with multiple missed opportunities. Your life is a façade.

The best formula is to acknowledge things as they come up and speak about them. This will mean a huge change for the faker, but change starts with a single decision. Gently but firmly you need to be repeatedly reminded that you have a right, both to assert your needs and to say NO whenever a request or demand feels unfair or excessive. By reinforcing a new and revised message that your wants and needs are legitimate and important, shows that it's safe to hold onto them even if they differ from someone else's.

Pretending to be someone you are not comes from a series of actions, such as:

- You compare yourself to others who are less fortunate or who do not have their act together and so feel better about yourself.
- You share only the good stuff or a version of it on social media. It is a perfectly curated story of your life that's not quite accurate. You also feel the need to over-share because the attention you receive online fills the void.
- You lie to yourself by not accepting your imperfections; they are kept hidden from others. Chances are you're hiding behind a disguise of heavy makeup, Botox, false bravado, and gadgets.
- You're afraid to challenge yourself and quit when things get tough; you give up and move on to the next thing. 'When the going gets tough, the tough get going'. Whether it's your career, fitness, or relationships

whenever a challenge comes along, you'd rather find something easier to tackle.
- You feel the need to brag to others. In social situations you tell modified or distorted stories about yourself that show how successful or lucky or admired you are.
- You don't take criticism well. Hearing anything contrary to the fake image you've constructed of yourself gets you really angry. Even when those close to you offer constructive feedback, you lash out in defence. Instead of listening and adjusting, you recoil further and further into your pretence.
- You criticise or put down others so that you can feel better about yourself. When friends or family experience something good in their lives, you aren't happy for them, instead you look for faults in them. When people are around you, they feel worse about themselves.

Acting like a fake, phoney or sham is a deception that stems from a lack of confidence and the fear that others will judge you negatively. It is also a protective device that gives only a semblance of security in a seemingly dangerous world. If you compare yourself to others all the time you will end up feeling much, much worse about yourself. The answer is not out there; it is within you. And if you start to backbite others in an effort to feel better about yourself, pause and say the good NO to yourself instead. Be authentic and see what happens.

STEREOTYPES

A stereotype is an inaccurate, over-generalisation about a particular category of people with reference to personality, preferences, appearance, ability etc. It is an expectation that includes every person in the category with no allowances for the uniqueness and diversity of individuals within the group. Stereotypes can be resistant to new information but they can sometimes be accurate as well. While such generalisations about groups of

Chapter 4: Healthy Mind and The Good No

people may be useful when making quick decisions, they are often inaccurate when applied to individuals and are among the reasons for developing narrow-mindedness, discrimination and prejudice. Stereotypes seriously interfere with a person being able to say the good NO when they ought.

Did you ever have the experience growing up where you were told by someone you looked up to that you had to be nice to others, especially your elders, no matter what. Or were you told something like, 'Come on stop crying, a nice girl like you doesn't look good when she cries, you'll make everyone else sad too… so stop it, dry your tears… it's not that bad'? If this denial of your hurt is repeated often enough you learn not to cry when you are hurt. Instead you put a smile on your dial and they all love that about you, thus the conditioning becomes embedded. It's not acceptable to show your true feelings and besides you get more positive reinforcement when you show that you are happy. That's how you start lying, first to those around you and then to yourself. You create a mask that's always automatically pleasant and smiley. You may also have been told, 'Do unto others, as they do unto you.' Another one is, 'If you have nothing nice to say, don't say anything at all' and 'Treat others the way you want to be treated.' Something parents will often remind children of is, 'Children should be seen and not heard,' 'Big boys don't cry' and 'Nice girls are more lovable.' These pronouncements are all designed to silence children and ensure that they do as they are told.

Boys and girls grow into men and women and these dictates follow them into their adult relationships. Common stereotypes that are perpetuated are:

- The man is the breadwinner of the family.
- All white Americans are brash and ignorant.
- Arabs are terrorists.

- Politicians are philanderers and think only of personal gain.
- Women are moody and changeable.
- The English complain all the time and have bad teeth.
- Football players are stupid.
- Women talk too much.
- The French are the best lovers.
- Australians are drunken loud-mouth racists.
- Men are strong and do all the physical work.
- Asians are good at maths and bad at driving.
- The Irish are drunkards and eat potatoes.
- The media exaggerate and tell lies.
- All blonds are stupid.
- Men only want one thing.
- All teenagers are antisocial.

What do we need to do to be seen as unique individuals rather than be typecast by stereotypes that are lazy interpretations of a person based on the superficial characteristics of a group? So are these stereotypes really fair? Stereotyping is the basis of prejudice; it can lead people to be driven by hate and suspicion, and can cause the victims of those stereotypes to be driven by fear and shame. It is a lose-lose situation, both for those who are perpetuating the stereotype through discrimination and those who are its victims. Xenophobia is the fear of strangers or of someone who is different from us. It typically involves the belief that there is a conflict between an in-group and an out-group. Can we really judge a person accurately from the outside and think we know them? Why is stereotyping so commonly practiced in our society if we know they can be inaccurate? How come no one is speaking out and saying NO to this?

Chapter 4: Healthy Mind and The Good No

TOXIC MASCULINITY

> Men tend to keep so much bottled up inside. This includes all the traumas and heart-breaking moments. Eventually there has to be a release. And too often that is in an explosive way.
>
> Ron Blake

The expression 'toxic masculinity' describes a form of gendered behaviour that focuses on the violence perpetrated by men. While gender identity is a deeply held feeling of what it means to be male, female or another gender, people of different genders often act differently. This is not necessarily because of biological characteristics but can be attributed to norms around what it means to be feminine and masculine. Yet, researchers have shown that there is very little difference between the brains of men and women. The Good Men Project defines toxic masculinity this way:

> Toxic masculinity is a narrow and repressive description of manhood, designating manhood as defined by violence, sex,

status and aggression. It's the cultural ideal of manliness, where strength is everything while emotions are a weakness; where sex and brutality are yardsticks by which men are measured, while supposedly 'feminine' traits - which can range from emotional vulnerability to simply not being hypersexual - are the means by which your status as 'man' can be taken away.

Toxic masculinity is a definition of manhood that is loaded with stereotypes around the way men behave such as men should not cry or admit weakness and men are just naturally aggressive. The term 'boys will be boys' is often heard when excusing a boy's behaviour, but this is just another way negative ideas are perpetuated around our expectations of boys. When a boy is energetic, thoughtless, rowdy, rude, hyperactive and destructive it's interpreted as being biologically wired as the rough and tumble of how boys are. As a consequence, boys are excused from any consequences for their behaviour and not held to account for their actions. When our culture buys into the idea that men are hardwired for aggression and violence, we excuse behaviours that hurt others physically and emotionally, and this starts in childhood. The Good Men Project encourages giving boys more credit by asking us to delete the 'boys will be boys' idea and saying NO to such labels.

Toxic masculinity involves cultural pressures for men to behave in certain ways and it's likely this affects all boys and all men to some degree. It refers to the notion that certain ideas of manliness perpetuate domination, homophobia, and aggression. The idea that men need to act tough and avoid showing their emotions can be detrimental in the long term to their mental and physical health, as well as, the serious consequences for society, which is how masculinity became known as 'toxic'. Toxic masculinity involves the extreme pressure some men feel to act in ways that are detrimental. Traditional characteristics that associate men as protectors, breadwinners or leaders, or that connects men with anger, selfishness,

Chapter 4: Healthy Mind and The Good No

and aggression are all problematic. These beliefs are common and are based on unproven biases that we, as both individuals and a society, perpetuate. Boys and men are taught to believe these stereotypes and are encouraged to measure up to them, ultimately harming themselves and others in the process.

Sarah Sheppard reports that researchers have come to agree that toxic masculinity has three core components:

1. Toughness: Being physically strong and muscled, emotionally callous and behaviourally aggressive.
2. Anti-femininity: This involves the idea that men should reject anything that is considered to be feminine, such as showing emotion or accepting help.
3. Power and Control: This is the assumption that men must work toward obtaining power and status so they can gain the respect and control of others.

Manhood, like womanhood, comes with many social expectations; we value kindness, compassion, and care in women more than we do in men. We also positively associate men with being protective and negatively associate men with being emotional. This does not mean that men aren't caring, compassionate or emotional but we, as a society, don't value these traits in men, and this can lead men to believe these traits aren't valuable either. When men actively avoid vulnerability, act on homophobic beliefs, ignore personal traumas, or exhibit prejudiced behaviours towards women, this contributes to many larger societal problems, such as gender-based violence, sexual assault, and gun violence.

Studies show that the more men conform to masculine norms, the more likely they were to engage in risky behaviours, such as heavy drinking and drug taking, gambling, fighting, smoking, reckless driving, and unhealthy eating. In addition, they were more likely to view such risky choices as normal. Toxic masculinity infers that it's inappropriate for men to talk about their feelings. Avoiding conversations about problems or emotions may increase feelings of isolation and loneliness, and reduce men's willingness to reach out and get help. Toxic masculinity views depression, anxiety, substance abuse issues, and other mental health problems as weaknesses, and discourages men from seeking treatment. It is commonplace to hear throw away comments and jokes from both men and women around gender stereotypes and it is this behaviour that reinforces the problem. Even more worrying is the way some parents indoctrinate their children into gender expectations. Saying NO to toxic masculinity is obvious. Try these:

'I feel offended when you speak like that, please don't do it again.'

'Your views are unacceptable and reinforce a serious social problem.'

'No, you weren't joking. In future think before you speak.'

'Don't talk to your child like that, if he doesn't want to play football, that's his decision.'

'That's not all right, man. Stop it now.'

▶▶▶

Chapter 5:
THE PEOPLE YOU CAN'T SAY NO TO

You don't develop courage by being happy in your relationships everyday. You develop it by surviving difficult times and challenging adversity.

Epicurus (341-270 BC)

The human psyche is deeply wired with a desire for connection and understanding. From birth we are neurologically primed to be in an intimate relationship and to seek out close bonds with others without which we would not survive. Most psychological and interpersonal difficulties stem from unfulfilled needs in these early relationships. For the most part, caregivers do their best but their own historical difficulties in relating and their ordinary human flaws mean they cannot be the perfect parent. Failures in connection and understanding are thus common experiences and most of us will experience the fallout from these failures at some point in our lives. The circumstances of childhood, such as the kind of family you are born into, have a major impact on the way you develop and grow. Your anxiety as a child may provoke an answering anxiety in your parents that may result in an escalation of your fears. Or you have internalised a message from your parents that they would rather you didn't show just how scared you really are because they cannot contain it for you. These childhood experiences interfere with the process of you knowing how to function in close relationships in a relatively uncomplicated way. This is where you can, for example, feel safe enough to trust that the other person will love you even if you reveal your flawed self, your fears, or your vulnerability.

Continuing, as you grow older you find that you do not have the capacity to turn to others in a straightforward way. You become worried about how you are perceived or judged. As an adult, the stories you tell lack authenticity and honesty as you increasingly feel the need to shape your self-image to suit the expectations of others and hide the way you feel. This is increasingly the case in a contemporary world where social media has become a dominant medium for connecting with others. Apps such as Facebook, Twitter, and Instagram encourage us to curate our images to the point that we often feel ashamed of our less than perfect characteristics. We are tempted to photoshop our images and present our lives as glamorous and fun, and our relationships as happy. We increasingly risk losing contact with what we can realistically expect from others and from ourselves.

Relationships

The ability to have connected and satisfying relationships is the most fundamental ingredient in securing some form of happiness. To have an intimate connection with others you need to be able to relate authentically. This requires two things: an honest engagement with yourself, and a commitment to becoming aware of, and taking responsibility for issues that may get in the way of this. You need to be open to your emotions and your vulnerability, and be willing to tangle with unpleasant and painful truths about yourself. This allows you to contemplate the ways you may unconsciously shape your relationships with others. You will then be able to make different choices in your adult life about how you relate to yourself and others that can fundamentally shift your experience creating space for you to be happier, more open and more genuine.

But what about relationships where the other person has been really tiresome for a very long time and you've just been putting up with it.

Chapter 5: The people you can't say NO to

They take up your time with their anxieties and hang-ups, they are always miserable and complaining, they never give you any quality time or put in an effort, they are envious of others including you, and they are passive-aggressive. They acknowledge you as their partner but they use you, never contribute to the family the same way you do, spend a lot more money than you do, they forget your birthday, cancel arrangements at the last minute, are unreliable, and they take, take, take, all the time with no reciprocation. You walk on eggshells around them and each encounter is nerve-wracking. You find yourself thinking bad thoughts about them and still you say nothing.

Take Stephanie's case in point. She is a classic people pleaser and fence sitter. She married her husband even though she had misgivings but didn't change her mind because it would create too much fuss. She persevered and tried to make a go of it learning early that she had to put up with her husband's bullying, his temperamental rages, his blaming her for everything, his mocking of her and his putdowns. They made a family together that included several children and she learned to tiptoe around him and give way for the sake of peace. She even told him she loved him when she was certain she didn't. She started to hate herself for not taking a stand but each time she spoke up it didn't make any difference, he never listened and she didn't insist. The years went by and she noticed that her life had become a sham as she pretended her way through each day. She hated going away with him on holidays because he would lose his temper all the time and make them all miserable. But at no point did she say I'm not going on holiday with you. She told herself she endured for the sake of the children, for the financial security and because of the punishment she feared her husband would level at her if she left. She was trapped and could see no way out. Her avoidance and passivity had turned her into someone she didn't like.

When someone fails you as a friend or a partner and you consider they are simply not worth the effort it takes to keep going, you have to stop and decide what to do about it. Something or nothing - if it's nothing then just keep going as you are, good luck with that! But if it's something, then what do you do about it? How do you proceed? What if this is someone who is so painful you dread each encounter? What if you are related or married and you feel you have to endure it because there are so many other connections to consider. Parents put pressure on their children to all get along with each other for the sake of peace. But this is not the kind of peace where there is going to be any harmony. And what if you have never ever told the problem person that they annoy you or that they should leave you alone or pay that loan back right now. You have let this behaviour go unchecked for such a long time. Boundaries have been violated and you did not protest, instead you neglected your own rights. In so doing, you will lose a friend or partner because of your own faintheartedness. Now you may want to be rid of the painful person but why were you friends with them in the first place. Why did Stephanie marry her husband when she had such doubts? She has to start thinking about her own part in the failure of that relationship.

Chapter 5: The people you can't say NO to

Internal struggles are common for us humans and are largely centred on the areas of self and intimacy and trust with others. The underlying issues are usually unconscious and so are outside of awareness, they, nonetheless, lead to patterns of behaviour that can leave you deeply troubled. How and why is this so? From where do they originate? What can you do about them? Psychoanalysis may be able to help you with this or you might want to start with some deep reflection first.

BAD FRIENDS

Sometimes a friend may puzzle you. You're not really sure about how loyal, supportive or genuine they are towards you. If you have a gut reaction telling you that your friendship isn't all it's cracked up to be, it may be time to discover what this person is really up to and whether this friend is worth keeping. Here are some examples of bad friends:

- The friend who tends to use you because you have assets like a car, a nice apartment, lots of money or a holiday house? Or, they may be using you to get close to someone else - your best friend, your partner or your brother or sister. This type of person has no genuine interest in you and will eat up all of your resources. Don't let that happen.
- The self-centred friend whose focus is always on themselves. They are definitely not good friend material; the world revolves around them and they do not have much space for you. You do favours for them and cut them a lot of slack but they never return the kindness.
- The 'poor me' friend who comes to you when they have problems or need advice, and lets you know, in no uncertain terms, how much hardship they are going through. But they are never there for you and, again, they do not give a damn about you.
- What about the insecure friend who doesn't want to share you with anyone else? They'll even squeeze themselves into relationships with

you and your best friend or your partner. And yet, they leave you out when they find a more important person to hang around with.

- The fake friend smiles in your face but when other people are around make you feel small by putting you down. They might promise to call you back but never do, and they always keep you waiting. They never keep their promises, they borrow money and never pay it back and their favourite hobby is to gossip. Give them a miss.
- The interloper friend uses you and your ideas or intellectual assets; they interfere with your social/professional contacts; they take over conversations you're having with others; they try to network and make friends with everyone you know; and generally climbs on you to get where you're going, rather than setting their own course. A user!
- The queen bee friend is really controlling and self-centred. She doesn't accept a differing opinion and only accepts you when you think/act as she does. She'll have her own entourage to endorse and defend her, look up to her, and worship her. Queen bees often take advantage of friendships and turn friends against each other, so steer clear.

You may be more tolerant of a questionable friend if they are going through a hard time so you may cut them some slack or give them the benefit of the doubt. But when the storm passes just wait and watch. Do they continue to mistreat you or walk all over you? Why do you allow this? Is it because you're pretending that it's not such a big deal or that you don't want to make a fuss? Or do you not want to seem like you're complaining or over-emotional? Have you ever been told that you are too sensitive or over-analysing a situation? Gaslighting occurs when the other person questions the veracity of your experience. It is a tactic to put you off kilter and manipulate your perspective on things so they get off scot-free. Do not buy into this approach. If

Chapter 5: The people you can't say NO to

you do nothing, you are inadvertently teaching them that it's okay to treat you that way. By reinforcing poor behaviour they will continue to do it to you and to others. Show some self-respect and put a limit on what you will and won't tolerate from others. Say NO. Think about what your expectations are of friendships. Do you have many good friends? What makes them a good friend in your eyes? Is there reciprocity between you? Are you tolerating bad friends because it's better than having no friends? Good friends are trustworthy, supportive, and respectful. They are simpatico with you. They have your back when the going gets tough.

Decide whether your friend is even worth keeping as an acquaintance. This will depend on the context, if you need to keep working with this person or seeing them at family get-togethers, then maintaining a calm and distanced acquaintanceship may be the best option. On the other hand, if this person has no other formal links to your life, you may wish to cut the bond entirely. If you are always the first one to contact a friend and you're getting tired of little to no response, stop contacting them. Block them from your contacts, and avoid seeing them in public. If this person is a friend, they will reach out if they notice they haven't heard from you, and it only takes a few minutes to text, email, or call someone. If they don't, you're wiser about this friend's attitude and you can begin to spend more time with the friends who do care. If you can't quietly distance yourself then you'll need to be up front about ceasing the friendship. The best way to break up with a friend who isn't working out is to meet them face-to-face or talk by phone, do not dump them via text or an email – that is spineless. Let them know in a crystal clear way that you feel unable to continue the friendship for such and such a reason. Use the good NO - avoid the use of blame language and do not assassinate their character. Just make it clear that this is about your feelings and your peace of mind. Wish them well.

THE FAMILY DRAMA

A kind of conspiracy frequently occurs in families where people want you to overlook someone else's repeated negative behaviour, for example, to let things go just this once for Dad's sake. This is a request for you to collude in avoiding a problem and be quiet for the sake of peace. Shut up and put up with it. In circumventing a confrontation the drama is avoided, at least for now, and the dreadful behaviour continues with everyone grimly enduring it. Propping up problematic people is peace at any price but the cost is usually the integrity of everyone involved. In a family this becomes a culture of collusion and manipulation aimed at controlling apparently unmanageable situations by doing nothing. Family members are shanghaied into subservience or held to ransom through guilt. It is often one senior family member who is in charge of controlling the emotional climate of a family and they influence all the others.

For Stephanie the crunch finally came when she couldn't stand to live the way she was living any longer. She told her husband clearly and without acrimony that she was separating from him and made plans to move out. He responded as she predicted but what she didn't expect was the negative reaction from her children where one refused to talk to his mother and the other became mean and argumentative. They couldn't

Chapter 5: The people you can't say NO to

forgive what they perceived as their mothers betrayal. Her decision to break up the family blind-sided them. In spite of it all, she felt at peace even though she had seriously rocked the boat, something she could never have imagined doing. But she has had to deal with the fall out and pick up the pieces. This may not have been so hard if she had been more forthright earlier in the marriage.

Being resolute is important particularly in the face of a family history that leans the other way. If you want anything to ever change with your family drama, short of you moving to Siberia, you will need to draw a line in the sand and stick to it with the good NO. But how can you do this with repeated bad behaviour by family members that include things like: getting very drunk/drugged, throwing punches or pulling hair, telling crude jokes and using foul language, lecherous intrusive behaviour, screaming and yelling, selling drugs to friends/family members, making small children cry, bullying others, poking fun at the old folk, and the biggest *faux pas* of them all, turning up with nothing, then eating and drinking their way through what everyone else has brought along, and leaving without helping out. Is any of this sounding familiar to you?

Repeatedly, people put up with this kind of problematic behaviour in families. They always forgive the offender and make excuses for him or her – he didn't know what he was doing, he didn't mean it, she was drunk and wasn't responsible, they were teasing him that's why he did it, he's going through a phase, she's been so depressed lately, he's never been the same since his girlfriend dumped him and on it goes. There is a litany of excuses as to why family members should tolerate the bad behaviour as though its normal, and they get sucked in each time hoping for a different outcome. This is how the drama is reinforced and becomes part of a family's mad story. Behind the scenes family members threaten never to put up with it again, but they do and are inevitably drawn back in. Besides they love each other and care about what happens. I'm not suggesting that there is an easy answer that pleases everyone or a quick fix that resolves things. However, at a certain point, for the sake of your honour, a boundary needs to be drawn.

Or you could go to the other extreme by excommunicating your family from your life. You rid yourself of them by imposing a boundary and ghosting them from your life. But when you walk away and never see them again you leave things unspoken and permanently unresolved. This is the supreme passive-aggressive act. That'll show you! This is as far away from the good NO as you can get. This is an extreme NO that lacks diplomacy and tact. There is no easy way out of a difficult family but if you erase them completely from your life you will never work out your own part in it. As a consequence you will carry undigested pieces of the damage you left behind with you wherever you go. And the people you left behind will have emotional responses to your rejecting them and cutting them off. And what if some day you realise that you made a giant mistake and you really miss these people you turned away from. They will never be able to trust you again even if they do welcome you back. But that would mean eating humble pie, wouldn't it.

Senior family members, usually your parents or grandparents, are the ones who hold authority in a family. It is because they hold the power that they can be central to a family's drama. A case in point is your mother who holds the notion of 'peace at any price' and makes sure everyone tows the line regarding this by deadening the family atmosphere and not reacting to anything. However, by overlooking continuous bad behaviour from your brother for the sake of peace she has made family life frustrating and oppressive. Delivering the good NO to a particular person means you also have to say it to the senior person as well. Be prepared to be out of favour with your mother even if she begs you to give way about your brother. The pressure will be terrible but if you persevere with the good NO your integrity will hold you steady. Standing up might mean offending your loved ones but remember they are pretty determined in this battle of wills to have you conform to their pretence of peace and forgiveness. So who is the real problem here?

Neither do you have to tolerate sarcasm, back-handed comments, mockery or sniping; the same goes for being talked over, shamed, and ganged up against. If you find yourself in these situations in your family just leave, go home, but tell them why you are leaving. If you are too emotional in the moment then tell them later but try not to leave it longer than a day. This is because it's so easy to just drop it. Letting it go maintains the dysfunctional situation. It encourages you to overlook it every time it happens and that ensures that the cycle will be repeated over and over. Even if you don't think it will make a difference remember not to underestimate yourself and the power of your words, especially your NO. It is possible to remain respectful of the people you love without getting roped into something you don't wish to be a part of. It is also fair and reasonable to expect that your family will accept your good NO choices. We tolerate a certain amount of rough and tumble in our families from which our resilience is built. But the real work comes with boundaries; your 'line in the sand' that is your limit over which you will not allow others to cross.

Standing up for yourself can be hard work, especially when you are just beginning. Just remember that you have rights, and you are not obliged to change or hide your lifestyle choices from those close to you. Nor do you have to accept requests to avoid discussing your sexual orientation in front of Grandma. You don't have to endure racist remarks about your flatmate or anti-Semitic comments about what's on the news either. Try saying something like: 'I'd like to believe that you don't understand the impact of that remark. So I hope you will reconsider and take it back'. Or stronger still: 'I fundamentally disagree with you and find your position offensive.'

Saying NO to your child

If you tend to give in to your child do you notice that they up the ante next time, and by raising the stakes they make it more difficult for you to say NO each time? They will take it to the ultimate place where you either give in or explode. It's the parent who is unable to uphold the good NO for the child. What is needed is a decision backed up by consistency where the child understands this is a good firm NO. It provides a sense of security because the child knows where they stand with you and that you have the strength of your convictions. If you have always given way and then suddenly say NO there will be a backlash. A wishy-washy NO does not cut it either. The child has taken it for granted that you are a pushover. Change is always hard in close relationships but if you can persist and develop consistency in your response they will get used to it, slowly, over time.

Some children can be like broken records that go round and round getting louder and more insistent each time upping the ante as they wear you down until they get what they want. The reason this becomes a problem is that the parent has conceded so many times they inadvertently reward their child for the annoying behaviour and now it has unfortunately become fixed. By the time the parent realises they need to instil a limit with their child their NO is ineffective. Kids are great at this because expectations of their behaviour are low. So now you have created a monster situation for yourself. Giving in for the sake of peace reinforces the problem and makes the setting of boundaries an insurmountable task. The only way to save the situation is to apply the 'counter broken record strategy' by not giving in at any cost. You say NO over and over and over. But first get outside help and make a parenting plan. Then speak to your child letting them know what you are doing and why. Listen to your child and answer their questions, even invite them in to the plan. Be resolute, be consistent and make sure you have back up.

Take caution here because to get their own way these kids have the capacity to hold their breath till they turn purple, refuse to eat and scream at such a high pitch your neighbours might call the police. How do you enforce a good NO in these circumstances? Like the family drama from which it has evolved, giving in for the sake of peace never works long term. Saying NO to your child is ultimately about raising caring, responsible, respectful children. Parental NO's are learning opportunities says Susan Newman and here's why:

1. **NO boosts your child's confidence.**

    Eliminate that first knee-jerk reaction to step in and save your child from discomfort. Instead, when your child asks you for help give him or her a chance to solve the problem themselves and feel proud of their effort. Your child can declare, 'I did it all by myself!' Listen and stop interfering when your child says, 'No, I can do it myself'.

2. **NO orients children toward a realistic view of the world.**

    Chances are, you will not be the only person to refuse your child. Strategic NO's reduce the chance that your child will feel entitled.

Among other advantages, refusals help children learn to handle disappointment and become resilient. They also help them sharpen their decision-making skills, tools they will need, as they get older.

3. **NO encourages children to be more self-aware.**

    Many children need to have that thing now without thinking about it. In the parents' quest to bring their children happiness, they give their child the thing whenever they want it. Thus, a problematic cycle emerges. The parents need to stop and put their heads together and think about what is best for the child.

    - Does my child really need to eat McDonald's tonight?
    - Does my son really need more extra-curricular activities?
    - Should we allow our daughter to spend the night at a friend's house when we are going away the next day?

    If you decide to refuse, discuss your concerns and the potential problems with them. This teaches your child to think critically about what they are doing.

4. **NO cultivates empathy.**

    For most parents, every task that's added to your child's calendar usually means you add something to your own to-do list. Most parents will agree that their children don't comprehend the level of commitment it requires to fulfil their child's wants and whims. Responding with NO challenges your children to recognise that you have needs too.

5. **NO helps teach money management.**

    Say your child wants an electronic gadget that his friends have and would like you to get it for him. Saying NO emphasises to the child that money does not grow on trees and maybe there are limited financial resources. You might suggest your son save up for the

Chapter 5: The people you can't say NO to

gadget by putting aside some of their pocket money or using their birthday money. NO can also be a handy teaching tool for teens who are working at their first job.

Once you accept the benefits of saying NO for yourself and your children, you will probably use it more frequently. Over time, you'll have less trouble standing strong in the face of your child's arguments and attempts to change your mind.

Chapter 6:
THOSE WHO WON'T TAKE NO FOR AN ANSWER

It's only by saying 'no' that you can concentrate on the things that are really important.

Steve Jobs

How do you practise The good NO in more challenging circumstances? These are situations when the other person ignores what you have said, they talk over you, they pretend they have not heard you, their talk gets louder and louder till they block you out, and in fact they will not take your NO for an answer. Anyone who disregards your right to reasonably refuse is someone who does not have your best interests at heart. You are not dealing with someone who wants to play fair. We have already agreed that human beings can be complicated, to say the least, and difficult people can make your life really, really hard. This is even worse if you are susceptible to being taken advantage of and are not in the habit of exercising your Good NO muscle. So the situation needs to be managed as best as you can. You can't do away with them but you need to deliberate on how you can extricate yourself from them, maybe permanently.

The good NO is well designed for bad behaviour. It says, 'I am not prepared to put up with that and this is what I am going to do about it'. Kornfeld declares that black-hole people are negative, rude, difficult, controlling people. They are pessimistic, drain energy, trigger the desire to flee, create conflict, feed off dramas, and are needy and moody. Start by knowing that there are many different kinds of people in the world and try to recognise and understand how they operate. This is so you can discover how to handle them appropriately. Information is knowledge and knowledge is power. So ask yourself some questions:

Do I feel annoyed or worried after I have spent time with this person?

Do they suck all the good energy out of the room?

Am I having trouble sleeping or having nightmares about them?

Do I feel drained or exhausted after I have contact with them?

Am I scared of them and the control they have over me?

Do I dread having anything to do with them?

Do I feel manipulated by them?

Do I hide to avoid them?

Am I afraid of saying NO to them because of the consequences?

Am I glad when they are gone?

The following are examples of the people who deserve to be on the receiving end of the good NO:

ONE-UPMANSHIP

One-upmanship is the practice of successively outdoing a competitor by upsetting them. Their one-upmanship is revealed in how they show you that they are better than you by always keeping one step ahead. One-upmanship folk are constant talkers and not interested in what you have to say; their only concern is for themselves and how well they can outdo you. They want to be heard and do not listen because they are always looking for opportunities to butt in. They are impervious to your needs and give you no personal space. As you edge away from them, they come in closer. They do not respond to non-verbal cues, so you just have to speak up for yourself, which means interrupting their monologue in order to say The good NO – bye-bye and exit quickly. This was exemplified in the Monty Python's Flying Circus skit called the 'Four Yorkshiremen', as follows (in a Yorkshire accent):

FOURTH YORKSHIREMAN:

I was happier then and I had nothin'. We used to live in this tiny old house with great big holes in the roof.

SECOND YORKSHIREMAN:

House! You were lucky to live in a house! We used to live in one room, all twenty-six of us, no furniture, 'alf the floor was missing, and we were all 'uddled together in one corner for fear of falling.

THIRD YORKSHIREMAN:

Eh, you were lucky to have a room! We used to have to live in t' corridor!

FIRST YORKSHIREMAN:

Oh, we used to dream of livin' in a corridor! Would ha' been a palace to us. We used to live in an old water tank on a rubbish tip. We got woke up every morning by having a load of rotting fish dumped all over us! House? Huh.

FOURTH YORKSHIREMAN:

Well, when I say 'house' it was only a hole in the ground covered by a sheet of tarpaulin, but it was a house to us.

SECOND YORKSHIREMAN:

We were evicted from our 'ole in the ground; we 'ad to go and live in a lake.

Chapter 6: Those who won't take No for an answer

THIRD YORKSHIREMAN:

You were lucky to have a lake! There were a hundred and fifty of us living in t' shoebox in t' middle o' road.

FIRST YORKSHIREMAN:

Cardboard box?

THIRD YORKSHIREMAN:

Aye.

FIRST YORKSHIREMAN:

You were lucky. We lived for three months in a paper bag in a septic tank. We used to have to get up at six in the morning, clean the paper bag, eat a crust of stale bread, go to work down t' mill, fourteen hours a day, week-in week-out, for sixpence a week, and when we got home our Dad would thrash us to sleep wi' his belt.

Narcissists and Control Freaks

The term narcissism comes from Greek mythology where a young man, Narcissus, falls in love with his own reflection. The narcissists you need to watch out for are seriously self-involved; their self-importance and entitlement mean they crave constant attention and acknowledgement from you. They do not care about you and have a limited capacity for care. If things don't go their way they will be cold, punishing, and withholding. When you are no longer useful to them they will drop you like a hot potato. Do not fall in love with a narcissist; they can be really mean and really cruel. Identify the kind of person you are dealing with early on. Remember your feelings are not such a good guide because narcissists can be charismatic and charming when they want something, plus they're often very good looking, unfortunately. Knowing yourself means you have the potential to know the other person or at least enough to question some of their motives. If you suspect a narcissist, cry a little bit and then run for your life!

Another version of the narcissist is the control freak; they obsessively try to dictate how you should feel in any given situation. They know it all; they're always right and can give you an opinion on anything. They will invalidate you, your opinions and your emotions. They gain control by dominating and demeaning. As a partner the control freak refuses to accept your independent point of view or the fact that you simply disagree with him or her. An illustration of this is 'mansplaining,' a pejorative term that shows what happens when a man over-confidently explains something in a condescending way, usually to a woman. His explanation is about something he has incomplete knowledge of, with the mistaken assumption that he knows more about it than the person he's talking to does.

For the control freak the idea that you might say NO to them is intolerable because that upsets the status quo. He, its most often a male, sets about developing conspiracy theories to explain why you are not cooperating with his version of reality. He is unable to accept that you are both two different people because it makes him very anxious to know that you do not think the same way. He needs the relationship to be a fusion where he is in control of the direction you will both travel together. Being controlled by a control freak is a nightmare for the nice person who tends to pedal faster and faster trying to satisfy the controllers ever-increasing demands. Negotiating does not work here; there is no other way but straight out the door and keep on going without looking back.

Emotional vampires

Emotional or psychic vampires drain the life out of you; they are high maintenance people who are exhausting to be around because they are always in some kind of tangle or catastrophe. Usually they suffer from poor judgment, neediness, pessimism and ineptitude. As a result, they

Chapter 6: Those who won't take No for an answer

need constant validation, they are self-defeating and nothing is ever their fault. Emotional vampires characterise themselves as victims and carry around a 'poor me' attitude; everything and everyone is against them and they demand that exceptions be made for them. They want your attention NOW. Potential solutions are met with 'Yes but I want YOU to do it for me.' Emotional vampires are stuck in self-defeating patterns of behaviour that make them hard going for the people they attach themselves to. Their excuses and excessive need for validation lead to antisocial behaviour. They get negative reactions from others who they, in turn, blame for treating them badly. This victimhood leads to an even deeper need for validation and so it goes on, inexorably. They suck the life out of people leaving them completely drained. Although, the ability for an emotional vampire to rationalise his or her antisocial behaviour is compelling, it's obvious that the reason they find life so hard is because of their temperament. As romantic partners emotional vampires are toxic, but they are everywhere, so you need to know how to shield yourself from them by setting clear firm limits. A necklace of garlic won't cut it.

The drama queen is a version of the emotional vampire; they turn every little thing into a major performance. They have a flair for upstaging everyone else in the 'mine is bigger or worse than yours' stakes. Perhaps you find yourself being easily dragged into other people's dramas. You step in to rescue them when they're in trouble. You're always at the other end of the phone from your drama queen friend. You're the go-to person in a crisis. Perhaps this is a role you've always played and when you meet new people, you're quickly pulled back into the role of fixer for someone else's crisis. Do not get caught up in someone else's histrionics. Be kind and do the good NO. Set limits and initiate consequences. Their sniffle turns into pneumonia as they tell you that their doctor said, 'It's the worst case he's ever seen'. They show up late for work because their car was towed away. The best response is, 'I'm sorry your car was towed away but you still have to get to work by 9am, your pay will be docked accordingly'.

People who go too far

Some people try to be tall by cutting off the heads of others.

—Paramahansa Yogananda

You might think control freaks, narcissists and emotional vampires are 'beyond the pale' but there are some people who are even worse than that. They are outside the bounds of generally accepted standards of civilised and legitimate behaviour. What they do is unacceptable, distasteful and downright wrong and the good NO will be a challenge in these circumstances.

Germany's invasion of Poland on 1 September 1939 is generally thought to be the trigger for the start of World War II. What follows is an excerpt from Winston Churchill's speech on 'The Defence of Freedom and Peace' broadcast on 16 October 1938 just a few weeks after the invasion. Churchill is inviting the world to stand up and say NO to Hitler:

> Dictatorship – the fetish worship of one man – is a passing phase. A state of society where men may not speak their minds, where children denounce their parents to the police, where a business man or small shopkeeper ruins his competitor by telling tales about his private opinions; such a state of society cannot long endure if brought into contact with the healthy outside world. The light of civilised progress with its tolerances and co-operation, with its dignities and joys, has often in the past been blotted out. But I hold the belief that we have now at last got far enough ahead of barbarism to control it, and to avert it, if only we realise what is afoot and make up our minds in time. We shall do it in the end. But how much harder our toil for every day's delay!

Chapter 6: Those who won't take No for an answer

Churchill's counsel to the people was to stop Hitler by being aware of what was happening and for them to make up their minds about what could be done. He was calling on the people to be decisive in recognising that it is the people who confer the power and authority onto a leader. So it is the people who decide not to go along with a problematic leader. What happened next is a common knowledge but here we want to know what to do about the dictators in our own lives. Churchill's advice is clear, be aware and decide for yourself.

When Russia invaded Ukraine at the beginning of 2022, Vladimir Putin delivered a chilling threat to the rest of the world over the imposition of sanctions on Russia. A defiant Putin warned that measures designed to cripple his country's economy were "akin to an act of war". He went on to arrogantly infer that the conflict could soon spread beyond Ukraine unless the west changed course. This use of intimidation is grandiose but possible. He is promising to teach the west a lesson and like all bullies he wants control. So with the Good NO in mind how do the people of the world even begin to respond to a threat like this?

In a string of phone calls from a besieged Kyiv, Ukraine's president, Volodymyr Zelenskiy, has persuaded the west to agree to a set of sanctions against Russia. Nations across the globe have imposed the largest ever package of sanctions against a major economy. Thousands have gathered in cities across the world to protest against Russia's invasion of Ukraine, calling upon their governments to take more action. The UK prime minister Boris Johnson said: "It is not enough to express our support for the rules-based international order we must defend it against a sustained attempt to rewrite the rules by military force. Putin must fail and must be seen to fail in this act of aggression." (The Guardian 6 March 2022) We shall see.

Habitual obedience to traditions, religious practices and customs are things that we grow up with in our families. Some rituals will have been more rigidly adhered to than others. Tyrannical people have a huge impact on their families, especially children. Typically, you grow up and when you leave your family you go out into the world to create a life of your own. But the deep roots of those early beliefs remain fixed in some of us and unchanged within our family. In these cases one or both parents or caregivers interfere with the child's capacity to grow up normally (here normal is relative) and that child replicates the family dysfunction in their own lives and the family they create.

Some parents, let's face it, it's usually the mother, have a hard time letting go. Perhaps they are over-invested in their child and have very few other interests. Or perhaps their desire to control and dominate is a way of preserving a fragile grip on their identity as a mother. Or perhaps their own parents were super controlling of them. Whatever the reason, they have forgotten the useful principle that from birth their job as a parent is to help their child let go a bit at a time as they negotiate their own way out into the world. For a mother who is unable to adapt to the changes in her children there will be consequences and none of them are pretty.

Unfair intrusions on those you seemingly love are present in all forms of relationships and are strongly linked to the behaviour of control freaks and narcissists. Abusers are in this category as well. Threatening, manipulating and guilt tripping your child into doing what you want is a serious problem. The quest for power and control fuel this kind of exploitation where supposed loved ones are undermined and forced into submission through continued white anting and gaslighting.

Chapter 6: Those who won't take No for an answer

Examples of this are:

> 'You'll be sorry when I'm dead. Then you'll know just how much I have sacrificed for you'.

> 'If you don't do as I say I'm going to tell them about what a terrible person you are'.

> 'Do as I say and don't ask any questions; I'm smarter than you are and I have your best interests at heart'.

> 'You are so ungrateful; after all I've done for you it's the least you can do for me.'

> 'You know I love you but sometimes…'

> 'If you leave me I will kill myself.'

You cannot change or control other people no matter how much you want them to be different. But you can look after and take care of yourself. Remember these few things:

You are in charge of you.

- Be very clear in your communications but keep it simple and brief.
- Always protect your boundaries even if you feel sorry for the other person, don't let him or her invade your personal space.
- Be choosy about who you open yourself up to. Avoid being vulnerable with tricky people.
- Do not absorb negativity, instead shake it off and walk away. Learn to detach and stay neutral.
- You cannot control how people interpret you or how they react to you.
- You are in control of safely extricating yourself from scary situations. If not, find someone you trust to help you.

- If you feel afraid of expressing yourself in your family or unsafe in standing up to your partner you need to find a way to leave in order to be safe. It is important for you to know that you cannot negotiate with terrorists.

Passive-Aggression

You teach people how to treat you by what you allow, what you stop and what you reinforce.

Tony Gaskins

Passive-aggression is a behaviour pattern of indirectly expressing negative feelings instead of openly addressing them. There is a disconnect between what a passive-aggressive person says and what he or she does.

What makes it confusing is that passive-aggression is manifest in a number of different ways, including the following:

- Resentment and opposition to the demands of others.

Chapter 6: Those who won't take No for an answer

- Procrastination and intentional mistakes in response to others' demands.
- A cynical, sullen or hostile attitude.
- Frequent complaints about feeling under appreciated or cheated.
- A pattern of passive hostility and an avoidance of direct communication.
- Some expressions of passive-aggressive behaviour include: sarcastic remarks and responses; being overly critical; temporary compliance; intentional inefficiency; allowing a problem to escalate through inaction or procrastination and taking pleasure in the resulting anguish; sneaky and deliberate actions taken in order to get revenge; complaints of injustice; and finally the silent treatment.

Passive-aggressive people regularly exhibit resistance to requests from friends and family by procrastinating, expressing sullenness, or acting stubborn. They give back-handed compliments; make others feel sorry for them, ignore what you say to them, and worst of all they are malicious and undermining. Passive-aggression typically comes in the form of a 'but' clause like, 'I don't want to sound mean, but…', 'I hope you don't think I'm insensitive but…', 'Not to be judgmental but…' after which they say something mean, insensitive or judgmental. They white ant or gaslight their way through workplaces and families, quietly eating away at the foundations.

Aggression is unambiguous. It's hard to misunderstand the meaning of a verbal missile or a punch on the nose. But passive-aggression is harder to grasp and it's worth getting a handle on how it operates in yourself and others. If you overly cater to the needs of others with little coming back in return you will progressively become resentful of the way you have become enslaved. This resentment accumulates so much influence over time that it inevitably leaks out in the form of passive-aggression. The anger you feel is not expressed directly but is deflected into apparently passive behaviour.

You can see it in the competitive colleague who would never confront you directly with a clear NO but instead 'accidentally' leave your name off an email about an important meeting as a way of sabotaging you. If someone points it out, you hear statements like, 'Oh, I had no idea' or 'I wonder how that happened'. Socially the behaviour typically comes in the form of backing out of an obligation at the last minute or giving an excuse that they can't make it when they had no intention of going in the first place. The symptoms look like deliberate inefficiency, an avoidance of responsibility or a refusal to state their needs or concerns directly. If you say, 'I'm upset with you about what you said' the passive-aggressive person will reply with … silence. It's always a go-to strategy for them because it says nothing at all and yet speaks volumes. It ostensibly avoids a conflict but in fact it provokes one with the very lack of communication serving as a taunt or a goad. It's thus passive, and yet challengingly aggressive.

The best solution is to limit the time you spend in their company. But if you decide that confrontation is the best path forward avoid being accusatory, just calmly explain how their behaviour has affected you. Good luck with that because they are not likely to care much and will not change their behaviour that easily. You will need to develop strategies to deal with these difficult people, especially if they are colleagues or family members. Remember that you cannot fix a difficult person so you will have to accept them exactly as they are by:

- Setting limits. Passive aggression can be a very damaging form of abuse. It's your right to set boundaries but the limits you set must be followed through. Make it clear with a good NO, that you won't tolerate being mistreated.
- Articulate consequences if they continue with the behaviour. Since passive-aggressive individuals operate covertly, they will almost always put up resistance when confronted on their behaviour. Denial,

excuse making, and finger pointing are just a few of the likely retorts. Regardless of what they say, declare what you're willing to do going forward. Importantly, offer one or more strong consequences to compel the passive-aggressive person to reconsider his or her behaviour. The ability to identify and assert consequence is one of the most powerful skills we can use to deal with a passive-aggressive person.

- Remain positive and calm while still being strong and firm about how much you are willing to tolerate. One of the biggest mistakes people make is being way too lenient and thus lose their options.

- If you care about this person and they are co-operative, help them figure out and address the root of the problem. Dig deep and honestly assess what might be driving the passive aggression. Passive-aggressive behaviour is usually a symptom of something else.

- If the person is passive-aggressive towards you on a regular basis, it is perfectly reasonable that you avoid them. Remember your own wellbeing is your priority. If they are not contributing anything significant besides negative energy, ask yourself whether it's worth having them around at all. Alternatively, find ways to spend only limited amounts of time with the person. Side step any one-on-one interactions with them and interact with them only when you are in a group. Determine when you might be able to avoid this person altogether.

- If you are passive-aggressive in your relationships with others the first step is to recognize this and make amends. Seek the assistance of someone wise who can help you understand what in your formative relationships might be reinforcing this behavior.

Aggression and Verbal Abuse

Aggression is a destructive form of communication that's associated with verbal abuse, which is the act of forcefully criticising, insulting or condemning someone. Aggression, bullying and verbal abuse are characterised by underlying resentment, anger and hostility that's expressed through threatening behaviour that's usually directed towards another person with the intention of harming them and producing negative emotions in them. It isn't the same as the normal conflict between people, such as having an argument or a fight or simply disliking someone. It's more about the repeated use of authority, perceived power or control over another person.

If you are going to deal effectively with aggression in others, it is important to understand and manage your own emotional responses. Some long-standing popular ideas hold that males are more aggressive than females, but research has shown that this is not necessarily the case. Women and men both use aggressive tactics but with women it's usually verbal and indirect as in passive aggression whereas men do resort to physical aggression more often. In workplaces, schools and in everyday life, a person who engages in aggression does so with the aim of gaining power over a targeted person, and to bond with others against the target. Usually, the aggressor knows no other way to connect emotionally with others and as a consequence they are feared, avoided and alienated.

Aggression is the inappropriate expression of anger that leads to loss of control as expressed in the following behaviours:

- Intimidation, bullying and violation of the rights of others in the form of yelling, screaming and using offensive language, as well as, name-calling and exaggerations – 'You are so stupid, it's all your fault'.
- A communication style that's verbally and/or physically threatening and abusive such as, accusing, blaming and attacking – 'You make me so angry.'

Chapter 6: Those who won't take No for an answer

- Focus is on dominating, humiliating or threatening others in order to manipulate and gain control over them through, for example, mocking or degrading jokes at another's expense.
- Impulsivity and a low frustration tolerance that's demonstrated in angry outbursts and temper tantrums.
- The use of aggression to criticise, blame and attack others to get their own way, as seen in judging and sarcasm – 'You think you're so smart, don't you'.
- Present as loud, demanding and overbearing. Giving orders and commands to exert control.
- Do not listen, frequently interrupt the other person, and use words as weapons characterised by blaming language and the use of threats and manipulation – 'If you don't get your act together I'm leaving'.

- Withholding, ignoring or withdrawing from the other person by blocking them out or denying the anger and abuse.
- Countering, discounting, minimising or trivialising the other person by refuting their opinion or experience – 'You don't know what you're talking about'.
- Gaslighting in a form of psychological abuse that denies the other person's reality, undermining them so they second-guess themselves or projecting guilt onto them – 'If you would only try harder'.

You need to get well away from people like this, as soon as possible; they are dangerous to be around. When your rights are being violated you know that you are in a problem situation that can escalate to a crisis. Do not fight fire with fire, it will only make things worse and spur the other person's aggression. Keep your cool and call for back up. Dial 000 if you feel you are in danger.

A few tips for staying calm in the face of aggression, even when you feel like you're bursting with anger yourself:

- Take a deep breath and try to keep your breathing regular.
- Do something else to diffuse the tension that's building up in the moment. Get a glass of water, open a window or take out your phone.
- Remind yourself of how much you will regret the things you might say out of anger.
- Don't go along with the conversation if it is bothering you. Calmly call it as you see it.
- Point out that the other person is being aggressive as an empathetic statement rather than agitating them even more.
- Your body language is important. Use an even unruffled tone. Maintain eye contact. Put your hands out with palms up as gesture of conciliation.

- Speaking clearly and firmly might help knock them off kilter especially if you do it early on. They may settle down and be more open to hearing what you have to say. Try something along the lines of:

    'There's no need to stress, we can work this out.'

    'Could you please lower your voice.'

    'Can I say something I believe might help?'

    'I understand this is upsetting for you.'

    'I'd like you to leave right now.'

Leave as soon as you can and remember not to be alone with this person again. Verbal abuse and intimidation are core elements in domestic violence that's perpetrated most often by men towards women. Intimate partner violence occurs in all countries and transcends social, economic, religious, and cultural groups.

Chapter 7:
How do you know what you are in control of?

What lies in our power to do, it lies in our power not to do.
                                                            Aristotle

You are responsible for yourself and the way you respond to unreasonable demands, intrusive impositions and audacious requests made by others that you do not want to accept even though you feel obliged to obey. When you give way to another person's unreasonable demands of you, you let yourself down. You are accountable to yourself for the consequences of your actions, or lack thereof. If you are aware of your vulnerability in this area it is a plus that you know this about yourself. You are also responsible for how you deal with guilt trips, requests to attend family functions you don't want to attend, inopportune times for a chat, reluctant hosting and visits you would rather not participate in. If you say NO to someone and they get angry it doesn't mean that you should have said Yes. It means you didn't do what they wanted you to do and they didn't like it. They did not like you saying NO to them and they may be way out of line. Learn that guilt and obligation are not very good reasons for saying Yes.

There is a Polish proverb *nie moj cyrk, nie moje malpy* that translates as 'Not my circus, not my monkeys.' This means that whatever it is, it's not my problem; it's none of my business. The mess that someone else has created is not your mess to clean up, and you have no control over the people taking part in that mess. However, in relationships questions

Chapter 7: How do you know what you are in control of?

around YES and NO need to be negotiated with a bit more give and take. Remember the preservation of relationships is important, especially if they are people you want to hang around with for a while.

Saying NO may be completely uncharted territory for you. When you are a master at saying Yes, you're bound to be a novice at the good NO. For you, saying NO means trying something entirely foreign. Think of this as an adventure into the unknown. To master saying NO, you may have to move out of your comfort zone and learn some new skills. While saying NO won't change your personality, it will help you assert yourself and put an end to that empty feeling in the pit of your stomach when you commit to things that are beyond your capacity or take you to the point where all your reserves are drained. Over time and with practice, NO will become your first option instead of a current, deeply ingrained propensity to say YES. You govern your own decision-making processes; how you deliver your messages, your response to the other person's reaction, and how you stand your ground when you deliver the good NO. If you can do that you have kicked a big goal in the 'being true to yourself' stakes. Those who refuse to accept your reasonable NO, and threaten you because of it, are real problems and your ongoing contact with them may need re-evaluation.

To ascertain what is within your control and what isn't, it's time to ask yourself some more questions about how well you know yourself:

- What are the consequences for you of saying NO and of saying Yes, both in the short term and the long term?
- What's the worst or best thing that can happen to you if you say NO? Weigh up the pros and cons honestly.
- Is it worth sucking it up or not?
- Can you negotiate terms?
- What are the benefits and costs of giving way and complying with each request that's made of you?
- Is this familiar? 'I can't be bothered with his drama, so I just give in because it's easier'. This needs a rethink.
- What are the benefits and costs of choosing what you want by saying NO?
- Is it possible to be less afraid of what the other person might do in response to your actions?
- After you have crossed the line and said NO it's too late anyway.

Develop some skills

At one time or another we all encounter tricky people whether it's in the family, socially, at work or in business situations, or even at the supermarket. Psychologist Andrew Fuller believes that handling bullies, backstabbers, white-anters, whingers and control freaks, blamers, tyrants, charmers, know-it-alls, perfectionists, competitors and the seriously self-obsessed well, can actually make you a better person. We all need imaginative yet practical ways of dealing with these risky and frustrating people, as well as, identifying the slippery techniques they employ to get their own way. It helps to understand relationship patterns, workplace politics, your own shortcomings in your dealings with others, and what a difficult person might be able to teach you. To manage low self-esteem, feelings of insecurity and inadequacy,

Chapter 7: How do you know what you are in control of?

anxiety and feelings of powerlessness people tend to engage in complicated behaviour. In fact, many of us behave in complex ways when we feel threatened.

The good NO is based on your ability to communicate with others, at least adequately. Interpersonal or communication skills are the behaviours and strategies you use to effectively interact with people. These skills range from the ability to speak and confer with others to non-verbal skills like listening, and a person's attitude or demeanour. If you're too direct or curt when you communicate the good NO you can come across as aggressive and this might put people off listening to you. If you show other people that you are listening to them, and that you understand them, they will be more willing to listen to you and accept your opinion.

For example:

'No, I'm passing on this. Thanks for thinking of me.'
'I agree that the night is still young, but no I'm not staying. Another time perhaps.'
'I see what you mean, it's a good point, but I still do not agree with you.'

Be aware of your language and use tact in how you express yourself. Where possible avoid unhelpful words, instead use positive words in a negative form. People react confidently to positive sounding words, even if they are used with a negative auxiliary.

Instead of: *I think that's a bad idea.*

Say: *I don't think that's such a good idea.*

In the same way, avoid finger-pointing statements that start with something like, 'You always …' this is aggressive and way too direct. Try to avoid saying 'you' and put the focus on 'I' or 'we'.

Instead of: *You're not listening to me.*
Say: *Perhaps I'm not making myself clear.*

Instead of: *You didn't explain the point properly.*
Say: *I don't understand your point.*

Sorry can be used in certain ways to interrupt, to apologise, to show you don't understand, or to disagree. It diffuses tension and it allows you to start a statement more comfortably. Use certain words to soften your statements but don't apologise for yourself – there is a subtle but distinct difference.

For example:
Sorry to interrupt you there but I have something to say.
Sorry but I still do not agree with you. I see things differently.
Sorry to override you but I think that's out of the question.
Sorry to disappoint you but I am not going.

Be assertive

Being assertive means expressing your point of view in a way that is clear and direct, while still respecting the other person's position. This is the essence of the Good NO. Assertiveness is a style of communication that many struggle to put into practice because of their confusion around exactly what it means. The mistake that's often made is the assumption that assertiveness means intimidation, control, rudeness, bossiness and so on – this is patently untrue. It's another myth. Synonyms for assertion are words like confident, decisive, firm, self-assured, positive, insistent, emphatic, sure, poised, self-reliant and self-possessed. Assertion is to be distinguished from aggression, passivity and passive aggression. The key to being assertive in your communication with others is to first learn how to manage your own emotions and uphold your boundaries.

Chapter 7: How do you know what you are in control of?

In any situation where your skills are being called upon remember to firstly stop and take a moment to gather yourself. Inhale deeply a few times to temporarily remove yourself from the situation before you react so that you can respond in a balanced way. When you are ready, calmly enter and address the other person directly while continuing to monitor your own responses. If you're delivering feedback or calling someone out on their behaviour, chances are this isn't the first time they've acted this way. But that doesn't mean it's a good idea to bring out the laundry list of past offences or make sweeping generalisations. Remember to keep calm, focused and to stay on target; don't get carried away. Also, remember the KIS principle – Keep It Simple. Communicating in an assertive manner can help you to:

- Minimise conflict
- Control your anger
- Have your needs better met
- Have more positive relationships with others

To implement the Good NO in an assertive way, rule number one is not to 'rise to the bait' by responding to provocations. Stay in the moment and use 'I' statements rather than 'you' statements. Maintain a boundary between yourself and the other person. Try to identify what you are feeling and think about why this might be. This is the know-how part of the good NO in the form of self- kNOwledge. Asserting yourself frees you from making shallow and insincere commitments, and it ensures you commit to things you can really put your heart into.

SET BOUNDARIES

Setting boundaries is an important part of establishing your identity; as a consequence it is a crucial aspect of your mental health and your

wellbeing. Boundaries can be physical or emotional, and they can range from being loose to rigid, with healthy boundaries somewhere in the middle. A boundary is the personal space between you and the other person; a clear line where you begin and the other person ends. The purpose of setting a boundary is to establish a protective limit between you and the other person. Transgressions are boundary violations that breach your rights and where permission has not been given. Signs of poor boundaries are:

- Letting others define you as in co-dependency
- Feeling guilty when you say NO
- Falling apart so that someone will take care of you
- Not speaking up when you need to
- Accepting sexual advances that you don't want
- Putting up with something that makes you feel bad
- Taking for the sake of taking

Chapter 7: How do you know what you are in control of?

- Giving till you're exhausted
- Expecting others to fulfil your needs automatically
- Touching someone without asking
- Going against personal values in order to please others

Establishing boundaries:

- Identify your 'no-go' zones. Boundaries and limits are non-negotiable and should be communicated evenly and clearly to others.
- Establish your boundaries by being the gatekeeper and guardian of your personal rights. Stand your ground when others push their perspectives onto you.
- Send out a clear 'no trespassing' message that if you violate this boundary there will be repercussions.
- Recognise that others may not always like what you say or do, but take the risk to speak up anyway. So what if they don't listen this time, the important thing is you have declared yourself. You cannot make people listen to you and the good NO may not change that.
- Deal with your guilt and manage your stress; the more you practise your NO the more relief you will start to feel. You are taking care of yourself when you say NO, and that's a good thing. Practice makes perfect!
- You are building stronger relationships when you set boundaries for yourself and, in turn, you must respect the limits of others.
- Represent yourself genuinely and take responsibility for yourself.
- Develop greater independence in your life.
- Never take without asking.
- Act with integrity as you consider how your behaviour might affect others.

The Good No

Upholding Your rights

Human rights are based on dignity, equality and mutual respect – regardless of your nationality, your religion or your beliefs. Your rights are about being treated fairly and treating others fairly, and having the ability to make choices about your own life.

Amnesty International

People often say, 'But I don't have the right to say no to this, do I?' Sure you do, you have rights. Australia, as in most countries, has national laws that protect the citizens' rights and freedoms, including your entitlement to being treated well in all areas of life. The doctrine of human rights has been highly influential in international law and government. The idea of human rights is said to be the common moral language of public discourse for a global society in peacetime. However, human rights advocates agree that sixty years after its issue, the Universal Declaration of Human Rights, is still more of a dream than reality. Violations exist in every part of the world all the time. Being entitled to rights does not necessarily mean that it happens; nonetheless violations of human rights should always be named and called out.

The invasion of privacy is an encroachment upon the right to be left alone or to be free from publicity. The law says it is an intrusion into the personal life of another without just cause. To breach a person's privacy is a criminal act. The law thus protects our right to privacy. That does not mean that breaches do not take place, they do all the time because the law has to be upheld. Upholding the law is similar to upholding the good NO. The law, like the good NO, is useless

Chapter 7: How do you know what you are in control of?

unless it is upheld, endorsed, protected, maintained and preserved. An important step in learning how to be more assertive is to identify your rights and make sure that your rights are respected in your everyday interactions, and to ensure that your own actions do not infringe on the rights of others.

So how do you uphold your rights? First know what some of your personal rights are:

1. I have the right to ask for what I want.
2. I have the right to say no to requests or demands I cannot meet.
3. I have the right to express my feelings - positive or negative.
4. I have the right to change my mind.
5. I have the right to make mistakes and not be perfect.
6. I have the right to follow my own values and standards.
7. I have the right to say no to anything when I feel I am not ready, it is unsafe, or it violates my values.
8. I have the right to determine my own priorities.
9. I have the right to not be responsible for others' behaviours, actions, feelings, or problems.
10. I have the right to expect honesty from others.
11. I have the right to be uniquely myself.

12. I have the right to feel scared and say, 'I'm afraid.'
13. I have the right to say, 'I don't know.'
14. I have the right to be in a non-abusive environment.
15. I have the right to have my needs and wants respected by others.
16. I have the right to be treated with dignity and respect.

A few basic good NO strategies are available to everyone in the form of protecting your rights and having clear boundaries. Setting boundaries can have a major impact on the quality of your life and peace of mind. Like your rights, boundaries have to be upheld. You need to recognise your own needs, desires and comfort zones and save your limited energy for those who deserve it. Start by standing up for yourself, stop agreeing to things you don't want, and don't feel guilty about putting yourself first or having a limit on unacceptable behaviour. Self-respect is reflected in the way you deal with others and the way you expect them to deal with you.

Do not use the good NO to avoid responsibility, punish another person or as a way of backing out of commitments. Use your No with integrity and as your guide to what you want. Remember there is nothing wrong with looking after yourself; it is not selfish to say NO to an unwelcome demand. In fact you will feel relief, as you begin to trust your ability to uphold your personal rights and stand up for yourself. People will always step over the line if they do not know where the boundary is.

Deal with your emotions

The world breaks everyone then some become strong at the broken places.

Ernest Hemingway

Chapter 7: How do you know what you are in control of?

We all have feelings or emotions. Some emotions are easier to identify such as joy and happiness and other emotions can be harder to deal with such as fear, anger, and sadness. This is why it is important to have the skills to address emotions that cause you distress, both in the short-term and long-term. Identifying a specific emotion can be complicated and more difficult than you may think. By recognising exactly what you're feeling, you begin to take away the power of an emotion's intensity as you work through what's caused it. Emotions reflect the ways your past and present have impacted you; they help train your ability to identify what is present in your life, based on what we've experienced in the past. Emotions tend to be fleeting, but allowing them to be there when they occur, listening to their message without clinging to them or defending against them, allows them to do their job.

Emotions unfold over stages, initially in response to a situation that you either consciously or unconsciously pay attention to, then you evaluate and interpret the situation for the emotional impact it's had. Your emotional response depends on your appraisal. The different strategies you use to deal with your emotions have different consequences. While some strategies are generally more helpful than others, there is no one best strategy to help you regulate your emotions. There are multiple ways of treating emotional distress or dysregulation, such as, relaxation techniques, mindfulness, grounding, cognitive behavioural therapy and meditation, to name just a few. You choose your own path to deal with your emotions.

Allowing yourself to feel vulnerable takes courage. When you feel yourself getting vulnerable, don't brace yourself or run away. Putting a wall up means that you continue to avoid what causes you to feel vulnerable and then you lose the opportunity to learn something about yourself and gain self-kNOwledge. Instead, take a deep breath and give yourself permission to experience your emotions as a consequence of being vulnerable, regardless of whether they feel good or bad. When you share a part of yourself with someone else you risk exposing yourself to rejection or indifference, and varying degrees of hurt. While that's not ideal, you know that you can probably bear it, lick your wounds and carry on. Another consequence of being vulnerable is that you risk being understood and accepted by someone else. When you make a conscious decision that what you're showing and offering other people is worthy, you extend yourself and show that you're worth their acceptance. So keep it up!

Brené Brown says that in order to courageously engage in our lives we need to embrace vulnerability and imperfection. Every day we experience the uncertainty, risks, and emotional exposure that define what it means to be vulnerable and thus all too human. Whether it's a new relationship, an important meeting, your creative process or a difficult family conversation, it is necessary to find the courage to allow vulnerability and engage with your whole self. Brown argues that vulnerability is not weakness, but rather our clearest path to courage, engagement, and meaningful connection. She said,

Chapter 7: How do you know what you are in control of?

> I can honestly say that nothing is as uncomfortable, dangerous, and hurtful as believing that I'm standing on the outside of my life looking in and wondering what it would be like if I had the courage to show up and let myself be seen.

People will usually respond to your vulnerability in a positive way because it indicates authenticity. Here is a genuine person who is taking a risk in being themselves. If you open up about your feelings, failures, and thoughts to someone you trust, you not only get reassurance and comfort, but you get another chance to practise being exposed and vulnerable. So in reality, allowing yourself to become vulnerable makes you stronger the more you practice it. The more often you show up just as you are, warts and all, the more chance you have of getting used to being yourself. You are unique, valuable, and important. No one else in this world can offer what you can or has the same potential that you have. You are a one-off original that cannot be replicated – make the most of it.

GROW YOUR SELF-DISCIPLINE

Skills, habits and all kinds of attitudes contribute to your individual achievements, but it is self-discipline that determines your success in life. Other words for self-discipline are willpower, self-control and self-determination. Self-discipline is the number one characteristic needed to successfully pursue your dreams and people with high levels of self-discipline are in general more confident and happier. So why do people lack self-discipline? The ability to be disciplined can be likened to a muscle; if it's not used or practised, it will weaken but when it's used continuously, it will grow strong. The more you exercise this mental muscle of self-discipline, the stronger your habit of being disciplined becomes. Self-discipline helps you achieve your goals and withstand the temptation of choosing the most comfortable option, which could take the form of a habit, an indulgence or the avoidance of something.

The sole purpose of self-discipline is to get you to your goal, no matter if it's pleasurable or not. Being a self-disciplined person is worthwhile because your reward will compensate you tenfold.

Self-discipline involves the following:

- The motivation to do the things that need to be done
- The resolve to overcome obstacles that stand in your way
- The persistence to keep going towards your goal
- The ability to train and manage your behaviour
- The mental capacity to regulate your feelings and thoughts

Giving in to temptations leads to a vicious circle. If you do not have the necessary willpower to withstand temptation, it'll be even more difficult to break the negative habit. A person who lacks a purpose for life will find it more difficult to maintain discipline. However, if you have a mission that you want to see realised, you'll be more likely to have the necessary willpower to pursue it. Start with something small so as not to lose motivation. This will not only help you get used to the new behaviour, but it

will also enable you to quickly reap the initial rewards as you gradually increase the exertion of your willpower muscle. As you master being disciplined in one aspect in your life, you will be able to add another thing you'd like to change as you transform your life one step at a time.

How to reinforce self-discipline:

1. Increase your stress tolerance levels. Higher levels of stress will lead you to make decisions that are instinct driven and based on short-term gratification. Stress management with relaxation, exercise, a good diet and sleep habits is important.
2. Meditation is one of the most effective methods to strengthen willpower. It increases self-awareness, concentration, focus, and attention, which allow you to make more beneficial decisions.
3. By eliminating temptations and distractions you do not even have to be more disciplined. All you need to do is to carefully remove these things from your life.
4. Postpone unbeneficial behaviours. If you want to break a bad habit it can be tremendously effective to simply postpone the activity. It will satisfy your craving to a certain degree, helping you to avoid it eventually. Delaying a cigarette puts you on the path to giving up.
5. If you do not eat properly, you're more likely to have poor concentration. This manifests itself as a weakened sense of discipline. Do what works for you.
6. Focus on identifying and removing negative habits. Make an active decision to change the habit and then put it to practice. Give it your best shot and stick to it.
7. Reward yourself. Think about possible gratifications for being disciplined. Treat yourself to something nice, as it will help you to maintain your motivation in the long run.

8. It is best to develop a clear plan. Write down exactly how you intend to be more disciplined and in what area of your life. Then outline the different steps you will need to accomplish your goal.
9. Learn to endure emotional discomfort. One reason we give in to temptation is that we try to avoid pain. However, it can be quite beneficial for you to tolerate a certain level of emotional discomfort. That's life.
10. Exercising regularly has been shown to increase willpower. It is also known to significantly increase your ability to withstand stress and distress.
11. Establish strong habits. Most habits are formed within 30 days. This might seem like a long time, but once something has turned into a habit, it is less likely to be an effort to practise it.

Resilience is not a trait that people either have or do not have. It involves behaviours, thoughts and actions that can be learned and developed in anyone over time. It is the ability to adapt and survive in the face of adversity, tragedy, threats or significant stress. Resilience requires strength and flexibility to recover from or adjust to loss, misfortune or change; it is where you bounce back from unexpected challenges in life; it is the facility to cope with tough times by applying inner strength and engaging support networks; it is about getting through pain and disappointment and not letting adversity crush your spirit. Like self discipline, resilience enables you to face difficult situations and cope better with challenges, as well as, helping improve your mental wellbeing. The foundations of resilience are laid down in childhood. What you are born into and how you negotiate childhood have a direct impact on how resilient or vulnerable you become. You can strengthen your capacity to deal with challenges but for some it requires more work than others.

Chapter 7: How do you know what you are in control of?

Shakira's pop ballad called 'No' was released in 2005. It explores a woman's efforts in trying to tell her boyfriend that she no longer wants to be involved in a toxic relationship with him and that separating is best for both. Here are the lyrics translated into English:

> No, don't try to apologize
> Don't play the game of persistence
> Excuses existed before you did
> No, don't look at me like before,
> Don't talk in plural
> Rhetoric is your most lethal weapon
> I'm going to ask you to never come back again
> I regret that you still can hurt me, here,
> Inside
> And that at your age you already know well
> What it's like to break someone's heart like this
> No, one can't live with so much venom
> The hope your love gave me
> No one else has given me
> I swear
> No, one can't live with so much venom
> One shouldn't devote the soul
> To collecting attempts
> Rage weighs more than cement
> I expect that you don't expect that I expect you
> After turning twenty-six
> Patience has sunk all the way down to my feet

The Good No

So here I pluck daisy petals
While I'm looking without seeing
To find out if you'll get irritated and leave
I'm going to ask you not to come back ever again
I regret that you still can hurt me, here,
Inside

Chapter 8:
Self-knowledge is the only answer

What a liberation to realize that the voice in my head is not who I am.
Who am I, then? The one who sees that.

Eckhart Tolle

Often, self-knowledge follows the path of introspection; it is concerned with being able to more accurately know the nature of your own mind in what you think and how you feel. Self-knowledge requires you to see yourself from a different perspective and to develop an understanding of how your mind and body react to the varied and complex experiences that go on in the world around you. To do this you need to experiment with thinking mindfully. This means, at least initially, processing your experiences free from judgment, interpretation and evaluation aiming to be awake and aware to the different moments of each day. When we are explorers, real listening appears automatically and in listening there is openness and receptivity.

As a child, you may have had strong ideas subtly implanted in your mind about what were normal and not normal things to experience. Within families prejudices and stereotypes around traditional expectations of boys and girls have an enormous influence on who you are and who you become. When difficult feelings threaten to emerge you take fright and flee so the focus is all over the place. By failing to investigate the recesses of your mind, you carefully protect a distorted self-image and you continue to think relatively well of yourself, at least some of the time. However, you don't get off that lightly. There is almost always a high price to pay for ignorance and unwillingness to look within. Feelings and desires that have not been examined and processed do not go away, they linger and spread their energy randomly onto neighbouring issues. Disavowed material strains the system and manifests in the form of symptoms, such as over-worrying, addiction, procrastination and physical symptoms like impotence, insomnia, headaches and on it goes. Being a stranger to yourself, you end up making bad choices: you leave a relationship that might have worked; you don't explore your professional talents in a timely way; you are negligent of your responsibilities; you lack insight into how you come across to others; and you alienate friends through erratic, off-putting behaviour.

The journey of self-realisation begins with self-study that leads to knowledge where eventually there is an understanding of meaning and purpose. Self-knowledge refers to the knowledge you have developed about the nature of who you are – your self. This involves a capacity for understanding aspects of your mind and the role it plays in shaping your behaviour. Early forms of self-knowledge prepare the way for later more complex forms to develop. As we have discovered, human beings are shaped very early by what happens to them. Through experience infants become aware of their own bodies and the effect their actions have on the physical and social environment. These effects become predictable and anticipated. Infants then become intentional in their actions and begin to read intention in the actions of others. They become self-reflective, learn to recognise their own image, and to form their life narrative. In the first few years of life, self-knowledge progresses from simple beginnings, with the help of an intuitive parent, to sophisticated forms of self-understanding that continue to grow throughout life, if enhanced.

Chapter 8: Self-knowledge is the only answer

Discernment

Be yourself! Everyone else is taken.

Dr Seuss

Are you so eager to keep the peace that your feathers get ruffled at the first sign of potential conflict? Is your concern about avoiding conflict causing you to turn yourself inside out to preserve peace? If so, you probably learned to be vigilant growing up in a particular kind of anxious family. Asking for other people's approval means you are giving up your own power. Being nice to people all the time can make you blind to the objective differences in people. In your desire to be completely non-judgmental, you can lose the ability to be discerning. Without the ability to discern, distinguish or discriminate you won't be able to get through life unscathed. This is because discernment is fundamental to choosing between certain options and making decisions, and decisions are what allow you to get through the demands of everyday life. Otherwise you can find yourself caught in a loop where nothing is settled on as a way forward and you stagnate. People pleasing is a way of relating to others that is deeply ingrained but that doesn't mean you can't alter it. When in doubt, its best to assume that other people's motives are aimed at being kind. Let them tell you if there's a problem, instead of trying to pre-emptively figure it out. Discernment is the ability to identify the small details, accurately recognise the difference between similar things, and then make shrewd decisions based on these observations. Discernment is the perceptiveness you show in being able to process the difference between what seems obscure and what seems obvious with awareness, insight and understanding.

Quit overcompensating in your relationships by doing more than you are supposed to or need to. Try to distinguish between what you may need to do and what you don't need to do. This is particularly so when it comes to children. It's best not to anticipate their every need, give them a chance to figure some things out on their own. Parents teach their children how to discern and differentiate between options. Discernment is the ability to tell things apart – to separate them, even when they appear to be very similar. People with discernment make keen observations about things because they listen, observe, assess and decide. Learn when to let things go if they are not all that important to you and identify when to take a stand if you ought to. Remember you have to pick your battles and not sweat the small stuff.

A person who learns to be both discerning and non-judgmental will experience the tremendous freedom of experiencing his or her true, authentic opinions about him or herself and others. Such a person will be motivated to look for a person's true talents, and of compassion towards those who haven't had success yet. Here are some tips that Harriet Braiker has come up with on how to be more discerning:

- Stop putting other people in charge of your important decisions.
- Tune in, take responsibility, and be the captain of your own ship.

Chapter 8: Self-knowledge is the only answer

- Snap out of it and take a sanity check. Ask yourself:
  - Are you standing on your head again?
  - Is what you're doing making sense?
  - Are you doing it this way because it's the way you've always done it?
  - Is it because that's how your parents did it?
  - Is it because others say it's the right way?!
  - What would an outsider have to say about what you are doing?
  - hat might they suggest?
- Consider taking a different perspective and contemplate what might be worth changing.
- Remember that looking for refuge in other people's opinions of you usually comes back to the fact that you don't think highly of yourself.
- Know that low self-esteem is a hallmark feature of people pleasing.
- Love does not have to be earned. Don't allow your worth to be tied up in what others do rather than who they are.
- Look at improving your relationship with yourself rather than fighting so hard for the approval of others.
- Practise compassion and be kind to yourself.
- Let go of things that do not serve you.
- Therapy helps too.

AUTHENTICITY

To be nobody but yourself - in a world that is doing its best, night and day, to make you somebody else – means to fight the hardest battle that any human being can fight; and never stop fighting.

E.E. Cummings

Do you hold back from telling someone how angry you feel with them, or not told someone you cared for that you loved them, or not talked openly about your sexual preferences with a partner, or not admitted to a mistake when you should have? You think you have good reasons to avoid being real, and in some cases you may, but much of the time you are fooling yourself about your reasons in order to avoid the stress and discomfort of being authentic. In the long run, however, you lose out if you continue to avoid being your true self. There is a difference between a values-driven life and an anxiety-driven life.

A values-driven life comes from what you value most and what influences your core beliefs around how you conduct yourself with others. If you are kind and considerate and see that all humans struggle you will treat others the way you'd like to be treated because it's the blueprint you live by. You choose to say NO, to take care of yourself, as well as others, and you choose to be assertive and honest without being aggressive and hurtful to others. The more authentic you are the braver you become, and the more comfortable you are in your own skin. The anxiety-driven life, on the other hand, makes being nice a way of managing anxiety. You learn to take a nice 'I'm happy if you're happy' stance as a way of avoiding conflict and confrontation. This means that you do whatever you need to avoid getting the other person disgruntled or upset because it makes you feel anxious. You don't say NO and you won't allow others to say NO either. You can't bear to be in the same environment where someone else may trigger your anxiety by disturbing the universe and disagreeing, or asking a difficult question, or saying the good NO. You don't speak up, nor are you assertive or honest because you are afraid all the time. It's a psychological way you protect yourself from what seems like a scary world.

Authenticity requires you to be able to be yourself by overcoming your desire to fit in and be part of the crowd. The authentic person is not

Chapter 8: Self-knowledge is the only answer

necessarily fearless but is, at least, willing to experience their fear and have the courage to stand alone. Most people like to imagine that, in a similarly challenging situation, they too would stay firm and champion justice, even if others stood against them. The fact is that most of the time people do not rise to the occasion or do the right thing. Yet think of the people you most and least admire, and the chances are you will find that it is authenticity that differentiates those you respect from those you don't. Given just how much we value those who are authentic, how come we find it so difficult to be that way?

If you decide that you are tired of being so nice, it's time to stop living on autopilot and begin to make authentic choices for yourself by taking on the following changes:

1. **Slow down and think about how you really feel. Live mindfully.**

    You probably don't even realise how you feel a lot of the time. Rather than leaping in to volunteer your services to others, pause and take a few deep breaths, ask yourself whether you really want to do this or not. Stop and figure out what you truly want. Don't be afraid to say NO.

2. **Use your anger as information.**

    When you feel anger, irritation or resentment use it as a signal or as information that tells you what you need, what you don't like, or what you might desire. Then voice your anger by speaking up and representing yourself well with integrity and tact.

3. **Practise being more honest.**

    Honesty is all about the good NO; it involves setting boundaries that are central to the experience of intimacy. Change the superficial talk with your partner or best friend, and experiment with deeper conversations. Tell those close to you how you really feel rather than saying you are fine all the time.

4. **Use your symptoms as signs to let you know when you're overextended.**

   Having a binge, experiencing signs of burnout or being passive-aggressive are all signs that you are overlooking something. Symptoms are red flags that something is wrong. Are you being overly responsible, are you apologising for things you did not do or are you overstretched because you are doing too much for others? Speak up and say NO.

5. **Push back against the critical inner voices.**

   Your critical superego voice is switched on and when you try to change anything it will ramp up. You will feel guilty, you will feel anxious that the world will despise you and terrible things will happen. This flares up when you start to break your old habits and patterns. Take a few deep breaths, congratulate yourself, and move on. Keep going and hang in there!

Truly understanding yourself, your intimate patterns of behaviour and your repetitions is the first step to being free of them. But we humans often struggle to achieve this understanding alone. This is because our approach to relationships tends to be driven unconsciously. Do everything possible to heal the psychical wounds from your earlier life. Your avoidance patterns may have come into existence to help you manage certain vulnerabilities regarding your parents, for instance. To the degree that you can access those earlier hurts and scared parts of yourself, you need to work through these issues. You're all grown up now and have your own personal authority. Your inner security no longer hinges on placating and being nice to others. Even if you do manage to gain some understanding of your patterns, a more experiential recognition is generally required for you to practise and achieve meaningful change. The tentacles of the past are long and enduring so if you can't seem to resolve these issues on your own, it might be best to consider talking to a therapist you can trust or who is recommended to you.

PHILOSOPHY OF LIFE

In a general sense, philosophy is associated with wisdom, intellectual culture and a search for knowledge. All cultures and literate societies ask philosophical and ethical questions such as, 'what's the meaning of life', 'how am I to live a good life' and 'what is the nature of reality'. Philosophy goes back to ancient times – the Greeks with Plato and Socrates, Hindu and Buddhist philosophy, Ancient Egypt and Babylon to Confucius in China and Zen in Japan. Aboriginal spirituality is derived from a philosophy of the notion of the interconnectedness of the elements of the earth and the universe where people, plants and animals, landforms and celestial bodies are all interrelated. These relations and the knowledge of how they are interconnected are expressed in sacred stories or myths. We humans have always sought knowledge about higher matters in the pursuit of wisdom. The discovery of the ultimate meaning and essence of existence is the central purpose of philosophy.

A personal philosophy of life is a general vision or attitude you have towards your life and its purpose. It's your reason for being here on the planet. We all need a personal philosophy in life, because without it we risk wandering around aimlessly, or being distracted by random stimuli, or getting drawn to intrusive material that seduces, such as gambling, drugs and alcohol, the internet, etc. A philosophy can be like a path you follow on your life's journey or a way of seeing and interpreting the world and your part in it. You have a purpose in this world: your skills, your interests, your desires, your values and your history have made you the perfect candidate for something. All you have to do is find out what that is. It's a good idea for us to take some time out to think about your approach to spirituality or philosophy.

The people of Japan provide a good example with the concept of *ikigai*. They believe that everyone has an ikigai that is the key to a longer and more fulfilled life and gives them a reason to get out of bed each morning. For all of us our ikigai is different, but one thing we have in common is that we are all searching for meaning. When we spend our days feeling connected to what is meaningful to us, we live more fully, when we lose the connection, we feel despair. It is hidden deep inside each of us, and finding our ikigai requires patience. Once you discover your ikigai, pursuing it and nurturing it every day will bring meaning to your life.

THE 10 RULES OF IKIGAI

Stay active - don't retire

Take it slowly

Don't over fill your stomach

Surround yourself with good people

Get in shape for your next birthday

Smile

Reconnect with nature

Show gratitude

Live in the moment

Chapter 8: Self-knowledge is the only answer

HUMAN SUFFERING

There will always be people to blame or people you hold accountable for causing you injury: parents divorcing when you were five, being bullied at school, the untimely death of a loved one, a relationship ending in disaster, being sacked from a job, failing an exam, a child who is delinquent and the list goes on. The pain, suffering and the dissatisfaction of life are central to the human condition. Victor Frankl said that if you change your attitude you have a greater chance of finding a hopeful, higher meaning of life. Sometimes life is just not fair; we are exhausted and all we know are setbacks. Frankl says that we are prisoners of circumstance and that we cannot change what has happened but we can change our attitude towards it and see our suffering as a challenge. He survived the concentration camps of World War Two Europe and wrote about his experiences, finally developing a psychotherapeutic method. He says that the meaning of life, even in suffering and death, is found in every moment of living and in identifying a purpose in life that you can feel positive about.

In the view of existentialists, an individual's starting point is angst in the face of an apparently meaningless and absurd world. Existentialism asserts that people make decisions based on subjective meaning rather than pure rationality. The rejection of reason as the source of meaning is a common theme of existentialist thought, as is the focus on the anxiety and dread that we feel in the face of our own radical freedom and awareness of death. Similarly, the Buddha's first noble truth, *dukkha,* is described in English as 'life is suffering' but a more literal translation is 'life does not satisfy' or dissatisfaction. The Buddha taught that at the root of all kinds of dissatisfaction is craving and attachment. We go through life grasping at, or clinging to, what we think will gratify us and in avoiding what we dislike. To be free from attachments we need to say NO to what we crave, cling to or grasp onto.

The Buddha's second noble truth tells us that it is the grasping or clinging or avoidance that is the source of our dissatisfaction. We are like drowning people who reach for something floating by to save us then discover that what we've latched onto provides only momentary relief or temporary satisfaction. What we desire is never enough and never lasts. The third noble truth assures us there is another way to find an end to suffering. This is when we develop a happiness that is not dependent on external objects or life events but results from a cultivated state of mind. The eightfold path can be viewed as a guide for the relief of dissatisfaction and suffering. It can lead to health and wellbeing by avoiding the extremes of self-indulgence on the one hand and total self-denial on the other. The Buddha called the eightfold path the middle way that comprises the following:

- Right view or understanding by knowing the direction you are heading in.
- Right intentions – that means having the resolve to follow the path.
- Right (careful) speech is about what you say in not harming anyone with your words.

- Right (honourable) action refers to what you do and not harming anyone with your behaviour.
- Right livelihood is about how you live each day without harming yourself or others.
- Right effort is about focusing your energy on the task at hand with a good wholesome state of mind.
- Right mindfulness is awareness and discernment of your mind, feelings and body.
- Right concentration is dedication to practice and training.

These eight steps are linked to the areas of ethical conduct, discipline and wisdom that are founded in detachment, compassion and simplicity. It is hard to be just a neutral observer or to dabble in this approach; you need to practice the path regularly. Dissatisfaction is central to the human condition. Where there is joy, pain will follow; where there is pain we will try to escape it. Human beings are faced with hardships in life that will cause emotional distress and pain. We are not very good at resolving our problems because human suffering is hard to grasp. Life is unpredictable and death is inevitable for us all. So, the teaching of the noble truths and the eightfold path is that the means of finding liberation from suffering is always available, if you choose it.

Acceptance

We're born alone, we live alone, and we die alone. Only through our love and friendship can we create the illusion, for the moment, that we're not alone.

Orson Welles

Acceptance is akin to acquiescence; it is your acknowledgment of the reality of a given situation and it is your recognition of a process without attempting to change it or protest against it. Acceptance of failure, loss and defeat is part of life. No matter how hard you try, some people won't be responsive to you. If you're deciding whether to bring up a person's behaviour to them with the good NO, it can be helpful to do a quick cost-benefit analysis to figure out if it's worth making an effort to get them to change their ways. Acceptance is the key. Others also have the right to say NO back to you and that ought to be okay. Acknowledge that others also have boundaries so do not apply undue pressure on them to acquiesce to what you want. Treat them with the same respect that you expect and learn to tolerate the discomfort of nor getting what you want. As you have been dishing out the good NO you too have to learn to receive it. Ask yourself if your requests of others are reasonable? Reciprocity and genuineness are important in meaningful relationships between human beings. You can't always get what you want and sometimes all your best efforts do not bring you the desired result. So just accept it and take note of the following:

- It is what it is.
- Sometimes things just don't work out.
- Life is give and take – quid pro quo.
- Just suck it up.
- Move on.
- Let it go.
- Life's a bitch and then you die.
- Say goodbye.
- Such is life.
- C'est la vie. (That's life)
- Life is just a bowl of cherries.

Chapter 8: Self-knowledge is the only answer

Blogger Mark Manson argues that life's struggles give it meaning. His book published in 2016, 'The subtle art of not giving a Fuck' is a reaction to the self-help industry and what Manson sees as a culture of mindless positivity that isn't practical or helpful for the majority of people. The point he makes is that most of us struggle through life giving too much and caring too much in situations that do not deserve that much effort. We sweat the small stuff, like why that guy didn't smile back when I smiled, why they cancelled my favourite TV program, how come the weatherman got the forecast wrong and why didn't my coworker ask about my weekend. When we believe we are perpetually entitled to feel comfortable and happy then we are on the slippery slope to misery and stress overload. Indeed, the ability to reserve our care for only the most worthwhile situations would surely make life a whole lot easier. Then failure would be less scary, rejection would be less painful and unpleasant situations in general would be a lot easier to manage.

In Mason's opinion, developing the ability to control and manage the fucks you give is the essence of strength and integrity. We must craft and hone 'not giving a fuck' over the course of years and even decades, and like a fine wine, the care factor will age into a fine vintage, to only be uncorked and shared on the most special occasions. But sadly most of us become drawn into life's trivialities and unimportant dramas that suck the life out of us. Not giving a fuck does not mean being indifferent; it means accepting being different. To not give a fuck about adversity, you must first give a fuck about something more important than adversity. 'The point is this: we all must give a fuck about *something*, in order to *value* something. And to value something, we must reject what is *not* that something. To value X, we must reject non-X (p.170)'. We all have a limited amount of time and energy so pay attention to where and to whom you give them.

As we grow older and enter middle age, something else begins to change. Our energy levels drop and our identities solidify. We know who we are and we no longer have a desire to change what now seems inevitable in our lives. And this is liberating. We no longer need to care about everything. Life is simplified to just what it is and we accept it as it is. Finding something important and meaningful in your life is the most productive use of your time and energy. This is true because every life has problems associated with it and finding meaning in your life will help you sustain the effort needed to overcome the particular problems you face. Thus, we could say that the key to living a good life is saying the good NO to more things, so that you can give a fuck about the things that align with your personal values. Acceptance means surrendering to what is happening in any given moment and learning not to resist or hang on so tightly. Rather than giving up, it's about letting go.

Finale

I am the master of my fate; I am the captain of my soul.

William Henley

Chapter 8: Self-knowledge is the only answer

Consider the information offered in this book. Much of it overlaps and is repeated a number of times in different ways as its woven through the chapters. This is for a good reason because we human beings need repetition and reinforcement. Our attention spans are short and we easily forget things that are important; we deny reality and ignore possibilities. We overlook or reject truths and potential solutions, and we resist or refuse to know things differently. We miss the very point that is staring straight at us, right in front of our eyes and we still don't see it. Resistance has to do with a refusal to know something in the face of evidence. It is a force that opposes or retards action. Resistance is often coupled with denial.

You have been asked many questions in this book that will hopefully give you food for thought and reflection. As your thinking shifts and you allow yourself to integrate different ideas and if it challenges your status quo you will notice that your ability to challenge yourself increases. The good NO promotes living and surviving. Understanding something about your suffering gives you the chance to make choices that are well defined and worthwhile. Learning to think mindfully enhances your self-awareness and self-knowledge, and this reinforces your use of the good NO with kNOwing; the knowhow that's behind the NO.

Let's be honest this isn't rocket science. I have gathered evidence as to why the good NO is a good idea and ought to be taken notice of. The rest is up to you.

REFERENCES

1. AUSTRALIAN INSTITUTE of HEALTH and WELFARE (AIHW) (2020) *Alcohol, tobacco & other drugs in Australia.* https://www.aihw.gov.au/reports/alcohol/alcohol-tobacco-other-drugs-australia/ contents/impacts/health-impacts

2. AUSTRALIAN INSTITUTE of HEALTH and WELFARE (AIHW) (2020) *Mental Health,* https://www.aihw.gov.au/reports/australias-health/mental-health

3. AUSTRALIAN HUMAN RIGHTS COMMISSION (2021) *Human Rights,* https://humanrights.gov.au/quick-guide/12096

4. AUSTRALIAN HUMAN RIGHTS COMMISSION (November 2021) *Set the Standard: Report on the Independent Review into Commonwealth Parliamentary Workplaces*, Sydney Australia. https://humanrights.gov.au/set-standard-2021

5. BLIKMAN, CHANTALLE (accessed 2019) *How to stop saying yes when you want to say no.* Blog -Tiny Buddha. https://tinybuddha.com/blog/stop-saying-yes-want-say-no/

6. BOCOCK, ROBERT (2002) *Sigmund Freud* - Revised Edition, London & New York: Routledge

7. BOTTON, ALAIN DE (accessed March/April 2021) *The School of Life.* https://www.theschooloflife.com

8. BRAIKER, HARRIET (2002) *The disease to please: Curing the people-pleasing syndrome*, Europe: McGraw-Hill Education

9. BRITANNICA, THE EDITORS OF ENCYCLOPAEDIA (Accessed 11 March 2021) *The Superego,* Encyclopaedia Britannica, https:// www.britannica.com/science/superego

10. BROWN, BRENE (2016) *Daring Greatly: How the courage to be vulnerable transforms the way we live, love, parent, and lead,* New York: Penguin

11. CARNES, PATRICK (1992) *Don't call it love: Recovery from sexual addiction,* USA: Bantam

12. CHURCHILL, WINSTON S. (16 October 1938) *The defence of freedom and peace* (The Lights are Going Out) Broadcast From Churchill, Into Battle. London: Cassell.

13. EINZELGANGER (accessed Jun 19, 2020) *The power of 'No',* YouTube https://www.youtube.com/watch?v=LUjwv-eKV7w

14. EVANS, DYLAN (2005) *An introductory dictionary of Lacanian psychoanalysis,* London: Routledge.

15. FELITTI, VINCENT J (2004) *The origins of addiction: Evidence from the adverse childhood experiences Study,* San Diego, California

16. FRANKL, VIKTOR (1946/2006) *Mans search for meaning,* USA: Beacon Press.

17. FREUD, SIGMUND (1978) *The ego and the id and other works.* In J. Strachey (Ed. and Trans.), The Standard Edition of the Complete Psychological Works of Sigmund Freud, Vol. XIX (1923–26) London: Hogarth.

18. FREUD, SIGMUND (1959). *Inhibitions, symptoms and anxiety.* In J. Strachey (Ed. and Trans.), The Standard Edition of the Complete Psychological Works of Sigmund Freud, Vol. XX (1926). London: Hogarth.

19. FULLER, ANDREW (2009) *Tricky people: How to deal with horrible types before they ruin you life,* Sydney: Harper Collins.

20. GLASNER-EDWARDS, SUZETTE (2015) *The addiction recovery skills workbook,* California: New Harbinger.

21. GOOD MEN PROJECT (2021) *The conversation no one else is having,* https://goodmenproject.com/ featured-content/the-difference-between-toxic-masculinity-and-being-a-man-dg/

22. GURDJIE. (accessed April 2nd 2021) *The Fourth Way: Self-knowledge and Understanding,* http://gurdjiefffourthway.org/pdf/SELF-KNOWLEDGE%20AND%20UNDERSTANDING.pdf

23. HILL AL, MILLER E, SWITZER GE, et al. (2020*) Harmful masculinities among younger men in three countries*: Psychometric study of the Man Box Scale. Preventative Medicine.

24. JEFFERS, SUSAN (2006) *Feel the fear and do it anyway,* USA: Ballantine

25. JOSEPH, STEPHEN (accessed 25 Sep 2016) *Why being a fake is bad for you,* The Guardian - Life and style. https://www.theguardian.com/lifeandstyle/2016/sep/25/why-being-a-fake-is-bad-for-you

26. KABAT-ZINN, JON (2003) *Mindfulness-Based Stress Reduction* (MBSR), Constructivism in the Human Sciences; Denton pp.73-83.

27. KASL, CHARLOTTE (1990) *Women, sex, and addiction: A Search for Love and Power,* Boston: Ticknor & Fields.

28. KORNFELD, PETER (2014) *Emotional vampires in your life: dealing with difficult people*, Createspace Independent Publishing Platform.

29. KNIGHT, SARAH (2019) *F**K NO,* London: Quercus.

30. LACAN, JACQUES (1988) *The Ethics of Psychoanalysis,* London: W. W. Norton & Company.

31. MANDELA, NELSON (1995). *Long walk to freedom: the autobiography of Nelson Mandela.* Little Brown & Co.

32. MANSON, MARK (2015) *The subtle art of not giving a fuck,* USA: Harper One

33. MERRIAM-WEBSTER DICTIONARY ONLINE (www.Merriam-Webster.com)

34. MONTY PYTHON's FLYING CIRCUS (1974) 'Four Yorkshiremen', from the album *Live At Drury Lane.*

35. NEWMAN, SUSAN (2017) *The book of NO: 365 ways to say it and mean it – and stop people pleasing forever,* New York: Turner Publishing.

36. OAKLEY, BARBARA, KNAFO, ARIEL, MADHAVAN, GURUPRASAD & SLOAN WILSON, DAVID (2012) *Pathological altruism*, England: Oxford University Press.

37. ORLOFF, JUDITH (2017) *Emotional freedom: Liberate yourself from negative emotions and transform your life*, California: Sounds True.

38. PSYCH FORUMS (Feb 2012) *Sexual addiction* Blog. For all the women who can't say no, https://www.psychforums.com/ sexual-addiction/topic101803.html

39. PSYCHOLOGY TODAY (2021) *Anxiety*, https://www. psychologytoday.com/intl/basics/anxiety

40. QUORA (accessed July 28 2021) *Why is there an obsession with anti aging and being young*, Blog, https://www.quora.com/Why-is-there-an-obsession-with-anti-aging-and-being-young?share=1

41. RICHARD, CHARLENE (2013) *The art of saying 'no' with grace and respect*. England: Charlene Richard RSW.

42. RODGERS, RICHARD & HAMMERSTEIN, OSCAR (1943) *Cain't say no*, from the musical Oklahoma!.

43. SELTZER, LEON (1988) Paradoxical Strategies in Psychotherapy, USA: Wiley.

44. SHEPPARD, SARAH (2020) *The dangerous effects of toxic masculinity*, https://www. verywellmind.com/the-dangerous-mental-health-effects-of-toxic-masculinity-5073957

45. SIMONIS M, MANOCHA R, ONG JJ. (2016) *Female genital cosmetic surgery: a cross-sectional survey exploring knowledge, attitude and practice of general practitioners*, British Medical Journal, Open. September 1st 2016.

46. STRAKER, G & WINSHIP, J (2019) *The talking cure: Normal people, hidden struggles and the life-changing power of therapy*, Australia: Pan Macmillan.

47. TOLLE, ECKHART (1997) *The Power of now.* Vancouver: Namaste Publishing.

48. VICTORIAN COSMETIC INSTITUTE (accessed 2020) *Cosmetic surgery statistics Australia and around the world,* https://www.thevictoriancosmeticinstitute.com.au/2020/01/cosmetic-surgery-statistics-australia-around-the-world/

49. WIDMORE, MICHAEL (2014) *The ultimate guide on how to handle difficult people*: *Taming the beasts, New York: JNR* Publishing Group.

50. WORLD HEALTH ORGANISATION (2022*) Alcohol,* https://www.who.int/news-room/fact-sheets/detail/alcohol/

51. WORLD HEALTH ORGANISATION (2022) *Substance Abuse,* https://www.afro.who.int/health-topics/substance-abuse